EXPLORING SERIES

A FalconGuide® to Exploring Everglades National Park and the Surrounding Area

A Guide to Hiking, Biking, Paddling, and Viewing Wildlife in the Region

SECOND EDITION

ROGER L. HAMMER

T0313656

FALCONGUIDES

GUILFORD, CONNECTICUT
HELENA, MONTANA

An imprint of Rowman & Littlefield
Falcon, FalconGuides, and Outfit Your Mind are registered trademarks of Rowman & Littlefield.

Distributed by NATIONAL BOOK NETWORK

Copyright © 2005, 2016 by Rowman & Littlefield
Photos by Roger L. Hammer unless otherwise noted
Maps by Multi Mapping Ltd. © Rowman & Littlefield

British Library Cataloguing-in-Publication Information available

ISSN 1553-9598
ISBN 978-1-4930-1187-2 (paperback)
ISBN 978-1-4930-1949-6 (electronic)

∞™ The paper used in this publication meets the minimum requirements of American National Standard for Information Sciences—Permanence of Paper for Printed Library Materials, ANSI/NISO Z39.48-1992.

The author and Rowman & Littlefield assume no liability for accidents happening to, or injuries sustained by, readers who engage in the activities described in this book.

I was able to explore strange rivers in canoes and push through tall grass to hidden mounds and stare at birds from boats. I saw things I had only heard about and learned things I could have never known.

—Marjory Stoneman Douglas, upon publication of her book *The Everglades: River of Grass*, 1947

Contents

Barred owls are common in hammocks, cypress domes, and mangrove forests throughout the Everglades region.

Exploring Everglades Overview Map

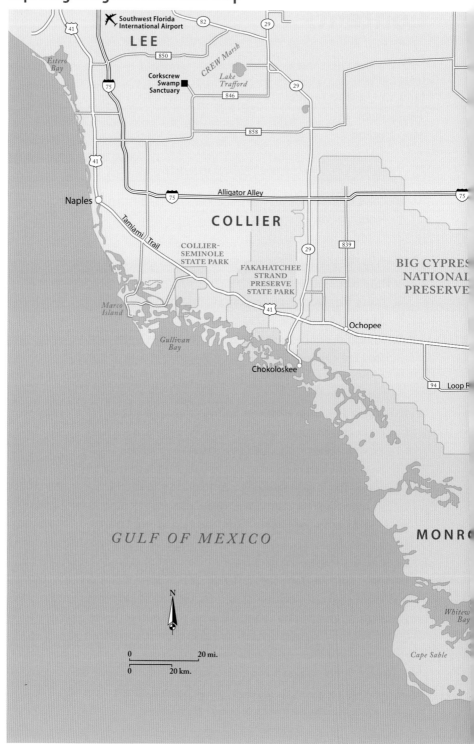

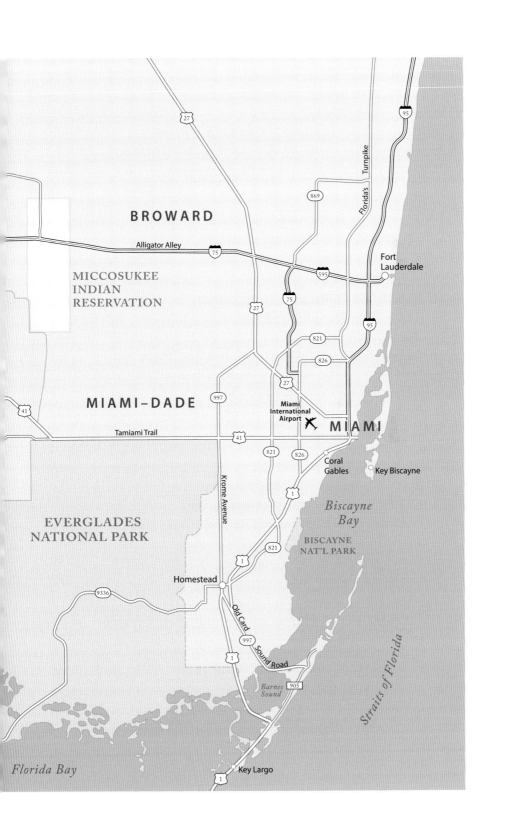

Help Us Keep This Guide Up to Date

Every effort has been made by the author and editors to make this guide as accurate and useful as possible. However, many things can change after a guide is published—water levels vary, trails and roads are rerouted, regulations change, techniques evolve, facilities come under new management, etc.

We welcome your comments concerning your experiences with this guide and how you feel it could be improved and kept up to date. While we may not be able to respond to all comments and suggestions, we'll take them to heart, and we'll also make certain to share them with the authors. Please send your comments and suggestions to the following address:

FalconGuides
Reader Response/Editorial Department
246 Goose Lane
Guilford, CT 06437

Or you may e-mail us at: editorial@falcon.com

Thanks for your input, and happy trails!

Hells Bay and Whitewater Bay offer some of the most beautiful, and at times daunting, paddling opportunities in Everglades National Park.

Preface

The Florida Everglades have not always been a tourist destination, as was so aptly conveyed in the writings of Harvard-educated army surgeon Jacob Rhett Motte in his diary from the Second Seminole War when, in 1837 at the age of 26, he penned, from *Journey Into Wilderness* (University Press of Florida, 1963):

> *After all, Florida is certainly the poorest country that ever two people quarreled for. The climate in the first place is objectionable; for even in winter, while persons further north were freezing, we were melting with heat. In the next place, the larger portion of Florida is a poor, sandy country in the north; and in the southern portions nearly all wet prairies and swamp; healthy in winter but sickly in summer; and in the south even the Indians said they could not live a month without suffering, and in summer not at all. It is in fact a most hideous region to live in; a perfect paradise for Indians, alligators, serpents, frogs, and every other kind of loathsome reptile.*

I first visited Everglades National Park in 1969. I drove the 38 miles from the main entrance west to Flamingo along the edge of Florida Bay and recall having a feeling of disillusionment because the Everglades were nothing like I had expected. I envisioned the Everglades being a densely wooded and eerie swamp with orchids, ferns, and vines draping from every available tree branch. I had somehow pictured a jungle like I had seen in Tarzan movies as a child. What I found were flooded grassy vistas that stretched to the horizon and rocky pinelands that were occasionally interrupted by dense forests of tropical, broad-leaved hardwood trees. This scenery changed rather abruptly to freshwater marsh dotted with stunted cypress trees and dome-shaped stands of taller cypress. Closer to Flamingo the landscape was overtaken by salt marsh and mangroves bordered by a muddy shoreline. Beyond the shore, sea-grass beds and countless mangrove islands stretched for miles across the shallow waters of Florida Bay.

Many years later I had the distinguished pleasure to visit the Everglades with the Grande Dame of the Everglades, Marjory Stoneman Douglas, and as we stood there gazing out across a boundless, watery prairie, I asked what she thought was so special about the view in front of us. She stood there silent for so long that I began to wonder if she'd heard my question, and then she quietly opined, "Do you hear that hawk calling for its mate? And did you see that flock of ibis that just landed in the cypress dome off in the distance?" And then tranquility overtook her again. Taking advantage of the silence that had descended upon her, I gazed back across the boundless expanse of Everglades, realizing only then that no more words were necessary.

It was only after reading *The Everglades: River of Grass* and other books about the region, coupled with countless more visits, that I began to gain even the most basic understanding of this unknowable place. Now, after more than thirty years of exploring the Everglades and paddling the 99-mile Everglades Wilderness Waterway three times solo, I can at least comprehend the pull of the place. The Everglades creep into your inner being and make you want to return even before the sore muscles, sunburn, scrapes, and bug bites have healed. The Everglades will never be fully understood, but that is why I keep returning. I hope you will too.

When humans first began exploring the Everglades more than 2,000 years ago, the place they saw was in its primal splendor. Water flowed unimpeded through central Florida's Kissimmee Valley into Lake Okeechobee. From there the water overflowed the lake's southern shore through a wide, shallow, vegetated marsh where it coursed southward at an imperceptible pace more than 100 miles to its final destination at Biscayne Bay, Florida Bay, and the Gulf of Mexico. Wildlife was exceptionally abundant, and birds numbering in the tens of millions decorated the sky. The Everglades were intact and functional.

The natural beauty and riches of the Everglades meant little to the first settlers and developers in Miami. They viewed the region as a vast watery hell and a frustrating hindrance to development. The foreboding swamp mocked them. This, however, would all change.

In 1905 Napoleon Bonaparte Broward was elected governor of Florida and it was he who ordered the first dredge—ironically named *Everglades*—to start the slow, arduous trek from Lake Okeechobee to the sea. This was the first effort, as Governor Broward put it, to drain the worthless swamp. In his pre-election political speeches, he pointedly proclaimed that other politicians were "draining the people and not the Everglades" and that "Yes, the Everglades is a swamp, but so was Chicago sixty years ago." In time much of the natural water flow was diverted directly into the sea and the Everglades began slowly drying and dying. During the next sixty years, more than 90 percent of the wading birds that nested in the Everglades disappeared. The future of the Everglades was precarious at best, but then came hope.

On Sunday, December 6, 1947, President Harry S. Truman stood on a palmetto-thatched platform at Everglades City in the northwest corner of the Everglades and proclaimed at the end of the ceremony to 10,000 onlookers, "Here we can truly understand what the Israelitish Psalmist meant when he sang: He maketh me to lie down in green pastures, He leadeth me beside the still waters, He restoreth my soul." For a moment there was unbroken silence, then applause thundered across the great swamp, the band played the national anthem, and with the stroke of a pen, the Everglades became an official national treasure. It was the first national park dedicated solely for its biological wealth, culminating years of lobbying and fund-raising by a group of staunch environmentalists dedicated to making Everglades National Park a reality. Sitting in the front row during the dedication ceremony was 57-year-old author Marjory Stoneman Douglas (1890–1998), whose timeless book *The Everglades: River of Grass* had just been published.

Today's Everglades are in danger from a host of problems, including toxic levels of mercury at all levels of the food chain, pollutants from residential and agricultural areas to the north and east, disruption of natural water flow by canals, levees, and roadways, insidious urban sprawl, and invasion by alien plants and animals. In a progressive effort to repair some of the mistakes of the past, on December 11, 2000, Congress passed the Water Resources Development Act, which appropriated $7.8 billion for a twenty-five-year Everglades restoration project. A wide bridge on Tamiami Trail (US 41) was completed in 2014 to allow a wide swath of water to flow unimpeded through the eastern Everglades region during the wet season. This and other projects are helping to place the Florida Everglades on the threshold of great changes and give renewed faith to those of us who love the place. It was perfectly fitting that President Barack Obama celebrated Earth Day in 2015 by visiting Everglades

National Park, where he spoke about climate change and the threat it poses to the Everglades and to the world.

I thank everyone who has ever been my companion on excursions into the Everglades, whether it was a day trip to look at birds or wildflowers, a kayak-fishing excursion on the flats of Florida Bay, or simply sitting on Cape Sable watching the tide flow in and the sun go down. Much appreciation goes to those who work at the parks and preserves covered in this book who took the time to review sections of the manuscript for accuracy. And a heartfelt thank-you really needs to go to all of the rangers and volunteers in the various national and state parks in Florida for their dedication. A special expression of gratitude also goes to Sonny Bass, Maryanne Biggar, Paul Marcellini, Vivian Oliva, Mike Owen, Larry Perez, Jimi Sadle, Bob Showler, Anne McCrary Sullivan, and Joe Wasilewski for their cherished friendship as well as their knowledge of the Everglades and things that live there. And a hearty thank-you goes to Bob DeGross, Chief of Interpretation and Public Affairs for the Big Cypress National Preserve, for commenting on the Big Cypress National Preserve section, and to Ed Talone of the Florida Trail Association for his firsthand information on the Big Cypress portion of the Florida National Scenic Trail.

My purpose in writing this book is to help you find your own special places to experience on your own terms—to meditate, reflect, or simply escape from city life to be close to nature. Exploring wilderness areas is a personal experience—one difficult to explain to others—and therein exists the mystery and charm of Florida's Everglades.

About the Second Edition

The second edition of this exploring guide has been improved in a number of ways: It is now in color, it offers GPS coordinates for trailheads, some new paddling routes in Everglades National Park have been added, and it now includes three paddling routes and camping opportunities within Biscayne National Park. Also, the book needed to be updated because when the first edition was published in spring 2005, it was only a matter of months before Hurricane Wilma struck southwest

Opportunities to view wildlife in the Everglades region abound at all times of the year.

Florida with 125-mile-per-hour sustained winds and devastating storm surges. The Category 3 storm killed twenty-five people and cut power to a record 3.2 million homes and businesses. Within Everglades National Park the storm damaged the motel and cabins at Flamingo so badly that they had to be demolished, and ten years later they still have yet to be rebuilt. The storm also cut in half Carl Ross Key, which was a popular camping destination south of Cape Sable in Florida Bay for canoeists and kayakers. Carl Ross Key has since been closed to camping and is only available for day use during part of the year. Two elevated chickees have been built in Florida Bay, one south and one east of Flamingo, that offer new camping destinations for wilderness explorers. The author and the publisher hope you find this new and improved guide useful in enhancing your experience while exploring this vast region. Happy exploring and be safe!

Introduction

The Everglades Region

Historically, the greater Everglades region covered some 13,000 square miles from Lake Okeechobee south to the Gulf of Mexico, Florida Bay, and Biscayne Bay, literally encompassing all of southern mainland Florida. Although the Everglades are the most famous of the Florida wetlands, the pre-drainage Everglades were complex and included the vast Big Cypress Swamp and the broad mangrove estuaries along the coastlines.

The popular term "River of Grass" oversimplifies the Everglades. They were, and still are, an interrelated ecosystem with distinct subregions, including broad prairies atop marl soils that typically were flooded only during the summer rainy season and deeper interior sloughs atop peaty soils that remained flooded in all but the driest years. Grasses and sedges dominated the true Everglades. Stretching southward along the inland edge of Biscayne Bay and then angling west into the heart of the Everglades was a wide, elevated ridge of limestone called the Miami Rock Ridge, which diverted much of the freshwater flow south and southwest through vast, open, grassy prairies. The Miami Rock Ridge was covered with seemingly endless pine forests that were occasionally interrupted by dense tropical hardwood forests called "hammocks."

When land finally gave way to the sea, the vegetation abruptly changed to coastal strand and tidal marsh behind a muddy shoreline rimmed by entangled forests of mangroves, which sometimes reached 20 miles inland. Creeks, bays, and islands dotted the southern coast, and great expanses of sea-grass meadows stretched across shallow, mud-bottomed bays between mainland Florida and the rocky Florida Keys. Together these habitats formed one vast ecosystem—the Everglades.

Southern Florida's terrain is remarkably flat. Much of it is just elevated enough to be called dry land. When referring to land in southern Florida, the key word is limestone, which is mainly Miami oolite that is either at the surface or just below a thin layer of soil. Miami oolite is sedimentary limestone that filtered out of shallow seas that once covered the southern peninsula some 130,000 to 120,000 years ago. It forms jagged outcroppings called "pinnacle rock" that make travel difficult. As flat as southern

Florida is, however, it takes only a slight decline in elevation to entirely change the natural landscape from dry, rocky pineland to open marsh with plants emerging from standing water.

Elevations on the Miami Rock Ridge average only 3 to 12 feet above sea level, declining imperceptibly toward the sea. Shallow, linear depressions that cut through the Miami Rock Ridge south of present-day Miami historically allowed surface water to flow through these openings. Some of it nourished Biscayne Bay but most of the flow was channeled into Florida Bay to the south and the Gulf of Mexico to the west.

Climate

Although southern Florida lies wholly in the temperate zone, it is closer to the equator and receives more rainfall between May and October than any other area in the continental United States. The climate is subtropical, with relatively mild, dry winters and hot, humid summers punctuated by heavy rainfall from frequent squalls and thunderstorms. Rainfall varies slightly from year to year, but the average for the southern mainland is about 60 inches annually, with most of it falling in summer. The annual rhythm of rainfall is sometimes dramatically interrupted by tropical storms and hurricanes that ply the Atlantic Ocean, the Caribbean Sea, and the Gulf of Mexico in summer and early fall. Rains can be torrential during these storms, and wind gusts can exceed 200 mph. November through April marks the dry season, when water is often depleted in much of the Everglades.

The warming effect of ocean breezes and the close proximity of the Gulf Stream, which passes only a few miles offshore of the southeastern coast, combine to create a favorable climate for tropical plant life and a winter destination for migratory birds. Because of pleasant winter temperatures, the Everglades receive the most visitors during this season, which is unfortunate. The summer rainy season is when the Everglades come alive with wildlife and wildflowers. It is only the hardy few, however, who truly appreciate summertime in the Everglades. Sweltering heat, high humidity, and insufferable swarms of the infamous Everglades mosquitoes can make life miserable, both for humans and for the animals that call the Everglades home. But the Everglades need to be seen during all seasons for one to gain even the most basic understanding of the exuberant life and enchanting beauty that make this land of mystery special.

Hazards and Health Warnings

There are, of course, plants and animals to be cautious of when visiting the Everglades. Three notable plants in the region have poisonous sap.

Poison ivy (*Toxicodendron radicans*) is a woody vine with three leaflets per leaf that are typically lobed but sometimes not. Simply brushing against the plant can cause a blistering skin rash on sensitive people, which usually appears after a 24-hour delay. Poison ivy is especially common in the Everglades region, so care should be taken to avoid this plant.

Poisonwood (*Metopium toxiferum*) has three to seven leaflets per leaf (usually five), and these are often marked with irregular black spots. Poisonwood is a shrub in pineland habitat, but it can become a large tree more than 50 feet tall in hammocks. Poisonwood can be very common along trails in Everglades National Park, where there are occasional interpretive signs warning the uninformed of its toxic nature. The sap can cause

The well-known poison ivy is common throughout the Everglades region.

Poisonwood may be a shrub or large tree and its sap can cause painful and persistent skin lesions. It is especially common in pineland and hardwood hammock habitats in Everglades National Park.

a similar, but often worse, skin rash to that of the related poison ivy. The trunk of mature poisonwood trees is light brown mottled with brownish orange and often marked by black blotches where the bark has peeled away in patches. There are products available that can be applied both before and after contact with either of these plants. If you are particularly susceptible to poison ivy, using these products may be helpful.

Manchineel produces sap that can cause temporary blindness along with severe skin and internal irritation. Eating the fruits can be fatal.

Another poisonous plant in the Everglades is manchineel (*Hippomane mancinella*), a state-listed endangered species related to the Christmas poinsettia. Within Everglades National Park it is locally common in the coastal hammocks around Flamingo, and there are some fine specimens growing along the edge of Buttonwood Canal near Coot Bay. Canoeists and kayakers paddling down Buttonwood Canal should be especially cautious of this tree. The leaves have long petioles (leaf stems), and the leaf blades have shallow serrations along the margins. The fruits are green and resemble small crab apples. The white sap is very irritating to the skin and can cause temporary blindness if conveyed to the eyes. Even rainwater dripping from the leaves is toxic enough to cause skin rash and burning of the eyes. The sap is water-soluble, so washing it off immediately after contact is advised. Eating the fruits can cause painful internal lesions and even death.

There are four venomous snakes in southern Florida: eastern diamondback rattlesnake, dusky pygmy rattlesnake, cottonmouth moccasin, and eastern coral snake. The best advice is to learn what these snakes look like (see the sidebar), treat them with deserved respect, and admire them from a safe distance. The same is true if you should encounter an adult American alligator (*Alligator mississippiensis*). Never approach large

Large alligators are known to kill people and pets in Florida, so they should be treated with due respect. Never swim where large alligators are known to occur and never attempt to feed one. The alligator pictured is at Anhinga Trail in Everglades National Park.

alligators even if they appear to be lethargic. Alligators can lunge forward and snap their jaw and tail sideways extremely fast. They can, and do, maim and kill people in Florida. The American crocodile (*Crocodylus acutus*) also is a resident of this region, and although there has only been one documented encounter with humans in Florida (a Miami couple swimming in a canal late at night in August 2014), large American crocodiles should be given a respectful berth. They are generally shy creatures except for those that have become accustomed to people, such as those around the Flamingo marina in Everglades National Park and in some Miami-Dade County marinas along Biscayne Bay.

Mosquitoes can be unbearable in some areas of the park in summer and fall, especially in coastal regions where salt-marsh mosquitoes flourish. Early settlers who once lived at Flamingo humorously proclaimed to tourists that in order to talk to one another in the summer, they had to throw a rock through the mosquitoes and yell through the hole! Another Everglades yarn has it that if you fall from a tree, either the mosquitoes or the humidity will break your fall. Anyone who has been around Flamingo

Venomous Snakes in the Everglades Region

Eastern diamondback rattlesnake *(Crotalus adamanteus)*: This beautiful snake is boldly marked with a pattern of light-centered dark diamonds with yellowish borders. There is a black, diagonal

line across the sides of the head and a facial pit between the eye and the nostril. It is the largest venomous snake in the United States and can reach 8 feet in length, but specimens more than 7 feet long are rare. So forget all the tall tales you've heard about 10-foot- and even 20-foot-long rattlesnakes in Florida. If confronted, the eastern diamondback will coil and face the intruder, usually announcing itself with a loud buzzing noise produced by the rattles at the end of its tail. This is a warning to intruders so admire it from a safe distance and leave it alone. Being bitten is a serious life-threatening medical emergency.

Dusky pygmy rattlesnake *(Sistrurus miliarius barbouri)*: This small snake is mostly brownish gray with a dorsal pattern of dark, irregular markings and a bright-brown stripe along its back. There are rattles at the tip of the tail, but the sound is hardly noticeable because of the small size. This snake is typically less than 2 feet in length but is very hot tempered. Being bitten is not life threatening but immediate medical attention is advised.

Cottonmouth moccasin *(Agkistrodon piscivorus)*: Young cottonmouths are colorfully marked with a bold pattern of dark, irregular cross bands on a brown or olive-brown body and a yellow tail. Older specimens are uniformly dark brownish black. There is a dark stripe along the side of the head and a facial pit between the eye and nostril. They  are thick-bodied snakes that can reach about 5 feet in length, but they are usually much smaller. Cottonmouths are very well camouflaged, so be especially cautious when exploring areas where this snake may occur. When confronted, cottonmouths will usually hold their ground (unlike most harmless water snakes). If threatened, a cottonmouth will throw its mouth wide open to reveal the white inner lining. This is a polite warning well worth heeding. Cottonmouth moccasins will not "attack" people as is often reported by sensationalists. Being bitten can be life threatening so seek immediate medical attention.

Eastern coral snake *(Micrurus fulvius fulvius)*: Coral snakes have a black head with a yellow headband and a body that is boldly banded with red, yellow, and black (the red bands are bordered by yellow). Harmless mimics such as the scarlet king snake have yellow and red bands separated by black. Remember the jingle *red on yellow, kill a fellow, red on black, friend of Jack*. This is a secretive and seldom-seen snake that prefers hardwood forests, where it crawls around in the leaf litter hunting other snakes and skinks for food. It must grab, hold on, and chew to introduce venom, so unless you pick one up or stand on one barefooted, there is very little chance of being bitten. The venom is neurotoxic and does not cause pain. Being bitten is a life-threatening medical emergency.

in summer can relate to these tall tales. Your best option is to wear long pants, long-sleeved shirt, closed shoes, and use repellent.

There are numerous brands of mosquito repellent on the market but a word of caution is in order. The active ingredient in most of these products is a chemical called deet for short. Products that contain 100 percent deet can cause severe, even fatal, allergic reactions in some people. Products that contain between 20 and 30 percent deet are effective and safer for use. Mesh bug jackets and head screens are helpful. "Organic" products that do not contain deet are largely ineffective when standing in the midst of summer swarms of Everglades mosquitoes, as are particular foods, diets, or electronic devices claimed by some to be effective. Those who choose to try these diets and gadgets quickly learn that running and screaming with arms flailing wildly is typically the end result. The good news is that mosquitoes are either nonexistent or reduced to tolerable levels from winter into spring.

Repelling mosquitoes is an important health issue in Florida due to the risk of contracting West Nile virus. This mosquito-transmitted disease has proven to be fatal in some cases, especially to the elderly and those with compromised immune systems. Other mosquito-transmitted diseases are malaria, encephalitis, dengue fever, chikungunya fever, and yellow fever. Not all of these diseases are currently present in Florida, but it is wise to use common sense and do not expose yourself to mosquitoes unnecessarily (especially freshwater mosquitoes). Other annoying insects in the Everglades include ticks, chiggers, sand flies (no-see-ums), deer-flies, and horseflies. Sand flies, deerflies, and horseflies can be especially hellish in spring and summer, driving people to near insanity. Allergic reactions to their bites simply add to the misery.

There is another health warning the reader should heed. High levels of mercury are found in many Everglades fish, especially freshwater species. People are advised not to eat largemouth bass caught south of Lake Okeechobee more than once a week. Young children and pregnant women should avoid eating them entirely (add alligator meat to this warning). The oscar, an exotic aquarium fish that has become established in the Everglades, has also tested high in mercury content. A mercury hot spot that backcountry fishermen should be aware of is Rookery Branch, an area northeast of Whitewater Bay that channels water flowing from the Shark River Slough to the Gulf of Mexico. The mercury level in largemouth bass, snook, and oscars is high in this region. A health warning also has been issued for spotted sea trout, gafftopsail catfish, bluefish, and jack crevalle caught in northern Florida Bay. Eating these fish periodically does not pose a health issue, plus consider that canned tuna is also high in mercury.

If you plan on fishing in salt water, there are a few fish that can cause you physical harm. Sharks, bluefish, mackerel, barracuda, and large snappers can cause bites that require medical attention or even hospitalization. Stingrays and spotted eagle rays have serrated spines near the base of the tail, and two species of saltwater catfish (hardhead and gafftopsail catfish) have sharp defensive spines on their dorsal and pectoral fins. These spines can cause excruciating pain that will likely require medical attention. This is also true of the recently introduced lionfish from the western Pacific Ocean, which can be found around offshore coral reefs and in Biscayne Bay within Biscayne National Park. Pain-relieving antibiotic ointments may be helpful for puncture wounds. Jellyfish and Portuguese man-of-war can cause severe and very painful stings, so treat the affected area with either ammonia or meat tenderizer that contains papain.

Habitats

The Everglades are a mosaic of interdependent plant communities. Depending on the season, many of these habitats may be dry or flooded, so count on getting your feet wet if you explore wetland habitats in the rainy season.

Pinelands

Two types of pineland occur in the Everglades: one with an understory dominated by saw palmetto (*Serenoa repens*) and another with a predominantly grassy understory. The slash pine (*Pinus elliottii*) is the single, dominant, overstory tree in South Florida pinelands. Beneath the tall, open pine canopy is a highly diverse ground layer of grasses, sedges, palms, vines, woody shrubs, and herbaceous wildflowers. Pineland habitat characterized by outcroppings of limestone on the Miami Rock Ridge is called "pine rockland." The principal upland area in Everglades National Park is Long Pine Key, which is nearly 20,000 acres of pine rockland interspersed by more than 120 tropical hardwood hammocks. Like much of the flora of southern Florida, most pine rockland plants have tropical affinities and occur only in the southernmost Florida counties. Others are endemic and occur nowhere else on Earth.

The pinelands of the northern Everglades region differ by having moist, sandy soils and a more temperate inventory of plants.

Tropical Hardwood Hammocks

Hammocks are dense forests of broad-leaved hardwood trees surrounded by a contrasting plant community, usually pineland, freshwater marsh, or even mangroves. They are shady, humid forests dominated by trees of tropical origin and resemble compact islands of trees. They occur on slightly elevated locations and are usually spared from fire because of the moist, partially decayed leaf litter and humid atmosphere that creates a microclimate within the understory. They are often associated with deep solution holes carved out of the limestone that hold water during the wet season.

Cypress Swamps and Mixed-Hardwood Swamps

Cypress swamps and mixed-hardwood swamps are the dominant features of the Everglades region north of Everglades National Park. Although flooded throughout much of the year, southern Florida's swamps are typically dry in winter and spring. As water in the aquifer rises during the rainy season, it soon saturates the soil and overland flow begins.

Cypress "domes" are rounded forests of cypress that form around deeper water than the surrounding area and can be seen throughout the Everglades region. Cypress "strands" are similar except they are linear in configuration and can be seen in the northern Everglades region. There are two species of cypress in the Everglades: Bald cypress (*Taxodium distichum*) is characterized by compound leaves with thin, linear segments that spread open like a bird feather, whereas pond cypress (*Taxodium ascendens*) has awl-shaped leaves that are appressed to the branchlets.

Mixed-hardwood swamps are characterized by cypress intermixed with a wide variety of temperate and tropical hardwood trees. Examples can be seen in the northern Everglades region.

Freshwater Marshes

The vast stretches of freshwater marshes throughout the Everglades region can be divided into swales, marl prairies, wet prairies, and sloughs (pronounced slews). Everglades swales are what Marjory Stoneman Douglas referred to in her book *The Everglades: River of Grass*, and this habitat is common in much of Everglades National Park. Swales have peaty soils and are dominated by saw grass (*Cladium jamaicense*), but most people refer to these as saw-grass prairies. Saw grass can form a vast monoculture in some areas. Marl prairies are formed above gray, claylike soils (marl) and are dominated by muhly grass (*Muhlenbergia capillaris* var. *filipes*) mixed with saw grass and an abundance of wildflowers. Both habitats are seasonally flooded.

Wet prairies are formed on sandy soils, and this is the prairie type seen in the northern Everglades region, especially around Corkscrew Swamp.

Salt Marsh

Salt-marsh habitat is generally found on marl soils of coastal areas that are inundated periodically by salt or brackish water, which allows the habitat to develop where mangroves are not dense enough to create an abundance of shade. Because salt-marsh plants must tolerate very salty soil, species diversity is lower than other plant communities. Watch for great southern white and eastern pygmy blue butterflies in this habitat.

Mangrove Forests

In the Everglades region mangroves occur along muddy and rocky shorelines of Florida Bay, Biscayne Bay, and the Gulf of Mexico in southern Florida. These forests are comprised of the red mangrove (*Rhizophora mangle*), black mangrove (*Avicennia germinans*), white mangrove (*Laguncularia racemosa*), and buttonwood (*Conocarpus erectus*). Mangrove forests are the most difficult of all plant communities to explore because of the arching maze of prop roots produced by red mangroves. They are also the least botanically diverse plant community in Florida but the most biologically diverse, serving as critical habitat for an astounding number of marine organisms as well as important nesting habitat for numerous species of birds. Mangrove buckeyes, mangrove skippers, mangrove cuckoos, and mangrove fox squirrels are associated with this habitat.

Beach Dunes

Beach dune plants are tough because they must be tolerant of dry, sandy soils, salt spray, and storm surges brought on by tropical storms. Natural beaches in the Everglades region occur at Cape Sable and Highland Beach in Everglades National Park; they are accessible only by canoe, kayak, sailboat, and powerboat. Key Biscayne, which is accessible by a causeway, is a sand barrier island between Biscayne Bay and the Straits of Florida.

How to Use This Guide

This guide offers information about the various trails and wilderness adventures available to visitors of Florida's Everglades and surrounding regions. It includes walking, hiking, backpacking, and biking trails, canoe and kayak trails and routes, and even places to explore in automobiles. There really is something for everyone in the Everglades region.

Some trails, especially wheelchair-accessible boardwalks, are easy and highly recommended for family excursions. Others may be moderately difficult but can be fun and rewarding for those interested in a more challenging adventure. But there are also trails such as the Florida National Scenic Trail for backpackers and the 99-mile Everglades Wilderness Waterway for paddling enthusiasts who relish real outdoor adventure and the experience that comes from dealing with unexpected events like rain, lightning, wind, waves, or strong tides. Experience and knowledge—not expensive gear and electronic gadgets—are what make outdoor exploring safer and more enjoyable. Weather and tidal conditions play a role in how difficult some paddling trails can be so always be prepared for the worst. Warnings about potential hazards or difficulties that you might encounter are offered in the text for each trail.

You will notice that mosquitoes and biting flies are listed as one of the special concerns for practically every trail in this guide. Summer and fall in the Everglades region can be extremely challenging, not only because of maddening swarms of mosquitoes and biting flies but also due to insufferable heat and humidity. Most visitors explore the Everglades region in late fall and winter—tourist season—when the temperature is generally comfortable, mosquitoes are either nonexistent or reduced to tolerable levels, and the heat and torrential rains of summer have subsided. But during the winter dry season, the cypress trees are without their beautiful green leaves and the open prairies are dry and rather bleak. Admittedly, wintertime is a very good season to be exploring the Everglades in relative comfort, and there are many wonderful sightseeing excursions available this time of year, but the Everglades are exciting to explore during all seasons. This book offers tips for summertime explorers too, because this is the season of high water when there is better accessibility to some backcountry areas that become dry in winter and spring. No matter what

Viewing birds up close from a canoe can create lasting memories of the Everglades.

season, it is hoped that this guide helps make your trip a fun, safe, and memorable one. Some of my most harrowing and grueling experiences paddling and exploring the Everglades backcountry are cherished equally as much as sitting on Cape Sable watching the sun go down and the tide come in. Hope to see you out there.

Trail Chapters

Individual trail chapters are designed to help you plan your own personal wilderness adventure. Each chapter includes the following information:

Trailhead GPS coordinates: These are offered for tech-savvy explorers.

Type of trail: The official uses of the trail (hiking, biking, canoeing, kayaking, or multiuse).

Type of adventure: A brief description of the type of adventure the trail offers.

Total distance: This gives you an idea of the distance of the trail, either one-way or round-trip, as well as distances between camping areas along the trail.

Charts: Some hiking and biking trails are indicated on maps that will make your trip easier to follow. For paddling trails available to canoeists and kayakers, this section also lists which nautical charts cover the region you are exploring.

Difficulty: This section informs readers about how demanding the trail or route might be to explore. Keep in mind that weather and tidal conditions can change the difficulty of canoeing and kayaking trails from moderate to strenuous in very short order. Also, some of the hiking trails can be more difficult when flooded or muddy. Difficulties also vary widely with the physical abilities and skills of each person.

Time required: This offers you a rough estimate of how long a reasonably fit person should take to complete the trail. This can vary greatly depending on your physical abilities or whether or not you wish to stop to observe wildlife, take photographs, or just hang out and relax. Photographers, wildflower enthusiasts, and birders will typically take much more time than someone who is just interested in hiking and sightseeing.

Special considerations: This section includes safety hazards, troublesome insects, poisonous plants, dangerous animals, and trail conditions that may be of concern. Hopefully none of these special concerns will keep you from enjoying your adventure.

Scenic value: This is a subjective rating of the overall aesthetic value of the habitats visible from the trail, but remember that beauty is in the eyes of the beholder.

Overview and Route Description: Here you will find a detailed description of each trail. The information will hopefully give you some insight on what wildlife and interesting plants you might expect to see as well as some good firsthand advice from an experienced explorer of the region. Some of the interesting human history of the area you are exploring might be mentioned, along with what types of fish you might catch if you are fishing in the backcountry. Alternate routes might also be discussed just in case you find yourself in a predicament you were not expecting.

Alternate route: There are some route descriptions in this guide that offer alternates for those who may want to take a shorter or longer trip. Alternate routes may also be useful if weather causes a sudden change in plans, especially for paddlers.

Trail Finder

Key to abbreviations:
ENP = Everglades National Park
BICY = Big Cypress National Preserve
BNP = Biscayne National Park

Best Hiking Trails
4. Long Pine Key Nature Trail (ENP)
18. Coastal Prairie Trail (ENP)
26. Elliott Key (BNP)
30. Gator Hook Trail (BICY)
33. Bear Island Unit (BICY)
41. CREW Marsh Trail—Gate 1
44. CREW Bird Rookery Swamp

Best Walking Trails
1. Anhinga Trail (ENP)
8. Mahogany Hammock boardwalk (ENP)
40. Corkscrew Swamp Sanctuary Boardwalk

Best Biking Trails
4. Long Pine Key Nature Trail (ENP)
35. Fakahatchee Strand Preserve State Park (Janes Memorial Scenic Drive)
39. Collier-Seminole State Park
42. CREW Cypress Dome Trail—Gate 5
44. CREW Bird Rookery Swamp

Best Paddling Trails and Routes
9. Nine Mile Pond (ENP)
11. Hells Bay Canoe Trail (ENP)
22. Everglades Wilderness Waterway (ENP)
24, 25, 26. Biscayne Bay (BNP)
34. Ten Thousand Islands (ENP) and Turner River (ENP-BICY)

Best Wildlife Viewing
1. Anhinga Trail (ENP)
13. Mrazek Pond (ENP)
17. Eco Pond (ENP)
23. Shark Valley (ENP)
32. Turner River Road (BICY)
40. Corkscrew Swamp Sanctuary Boardwalk

Best Wildflower Viewing
4. Long Pine Key Nature Trail (ENP)
33. Bear Island Unit (BICY)
38. Collier-Seminole State Park
41. CREW Marsh Trails

Best Primitive Tent Camping
19. Cape Sable (ENP)
22. Everglades Wilderness Waterway (ENP)
22. Pavilion Key (ENP)
33. Bear Island Unit (BICY)
37. Collier-Seminole State Park

Best Wheelchair-Accessible Trails and Tours
1. Anhinga Trail (ENP)
2. Gumbo Limbo Trail (ENP)
7. Pa-Hay-Okee (ENP)
8. Mahogany Hammock boardwalk (ENP)
23. Shark Valley (ENP)
40. Corkscrew Swamp Sanctuary Boardwalk

Other accessible excursions in the area include guided boat tours that leave out of Flamingo to Whitewater Bay and Florida Bay and the boardwalk along Tamiami Canal at the Oasis Visitor Center.

Map Legend

〔75〕	Interstate Highway	✈	Airport
〔41〕	US Highway	▲	Campground
〔29〕	State Highway	▲	Campsite
〔94〕	County/Forest Road	○	City
	Local Road		Gate
= = = = =	Unimproved Road	🅿	Parking
	Featured Road	🧺	Picnic Area
- - - - - •	Featured Trail	■	Point of Interest
- - - - - - -	Trail		Ranger Station
‖‖‖‖‖‖	Boardwalk		Scenic View/Viewpoint
	Bluff/Cliff		Tower
	Small River or Creek	○	Town
	Marsh/Swamp	◇10◇	Trail Junction/Mileage Marker
	Mangrove	①	Trailhead
	Body of Water	❓	Visitor/Information Center
	National Forest/Park		
	National Preserve/ Preserve State Park		

Everglades National Park, Main Entrance

40001 SR 9336
Homestead, FL 33034
Main office: (305) 242-7700
Ernest F. Coe Visitor Center: (305) 242-7700
Flamingo Visitor Center: (239) 695-2945 (staffed intermittently in summer)
Shark Valley Visitor Center: (305) 221-8776
Gulf Coast Visitor Center: (239) 695-3311
24-hour Emergency Dispatch: (305) 242-7740
Website: nps.gov/ever

> *Buffaloes are grand, but name another park that harbors panthers at one end and hammerhead sharks at the other.*
> —Carl Hiaasen, "Everglades National Park Fiftieth Anniversary: Homage to a Magical Place,"
> *Miami Herald*, October 19, 1997

THE MAIN ENTRANCE INTO EVERGLADES NATIONAL PARK IS WEST OF Homestead and Florida City. There are ample motel accommodations and restaurants along US 1 and Krome Avenue (SW 177th Avenue; SR 997) in both cities. Be advised that the motel and cabins at Flamingo were destroyed by Hurricane Wilma in 2005 and have not yet been rebuilt. Tent camping and recreational vehicle (RV) facilities are available inside the park at Long Pine Key and Flamingo. Long Pine Key and Flamingo can both be accessed from the main park road (SR 9336).

The park's main entrance is easily accessible from the Florida Turnpike (Homestead Extension) by continuing south to its terminus at US 1 in Florida City. A sign above the off-ramp will direct you to turn right onto Palm Drive (SW 344th Street). Continue west to SW 192nd Avenue, where you will see the Robert Is Here fruit stand. Turn left and continue to SR 9336, turn right, and continue west to the park entrance.

Everglades National Park, Main Entrance

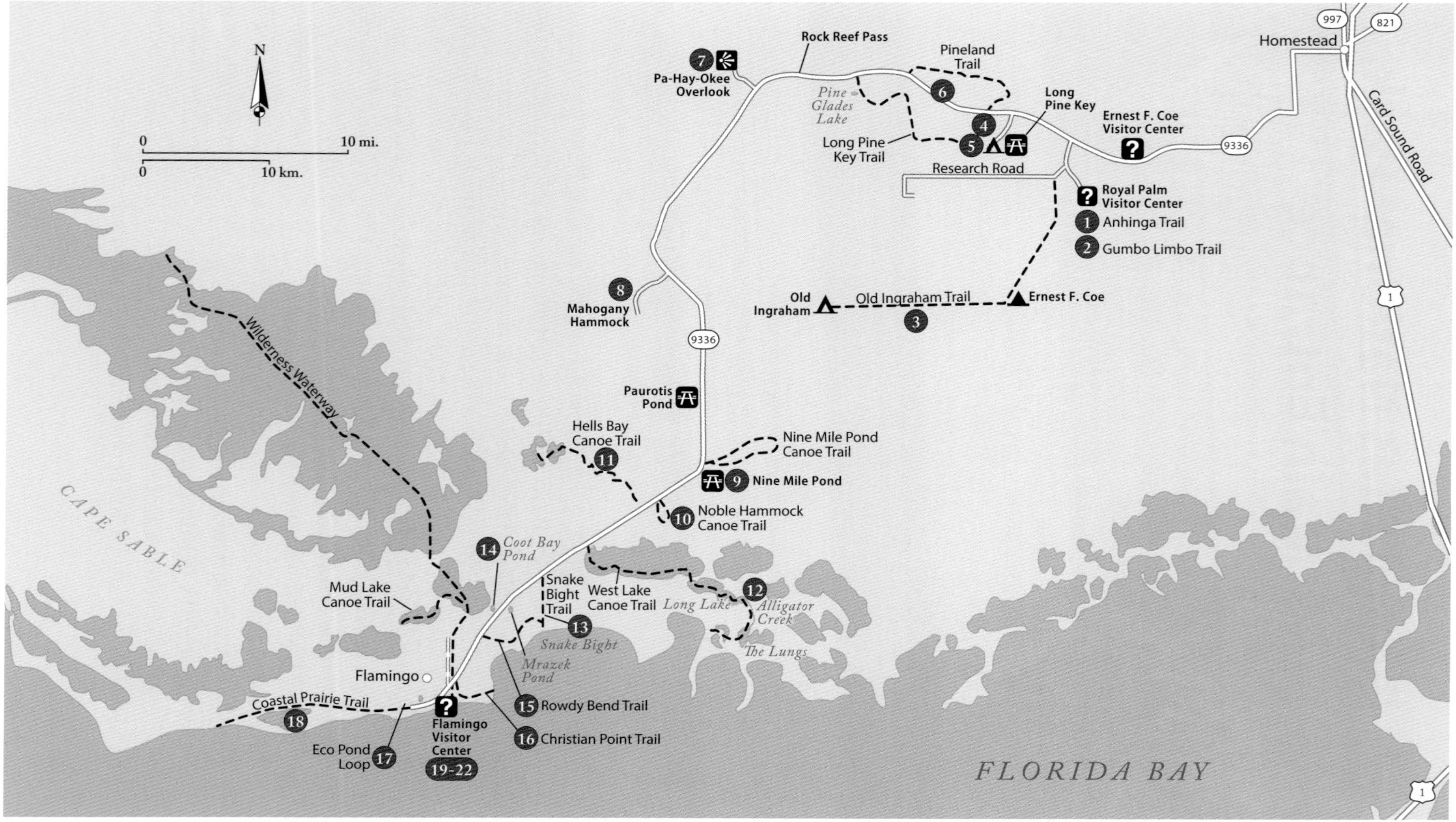

Card Sound Road

Homestead

FLORIDA BAY

Ernest F. Coe Visitor Center

Long Pine Key

Royal Palm Visitor Center

1 Anhinga Trail
2 Gumbo Limbo Trail

Ernest F. Coe

Pineland Trail

Research Road

Old Ingraham Trail

4
5
6

Rock Reef Pass

Pine Glades Lake

Long Pine Key Trail

Old Ingraham

3

7 Pa-Hay-Okee Overlook

8 Mahogany Hammock

Nine Mile Pond Canoe Trail

9 Nine Mile Pond

Noble Hammock Canoe Trail

10

Paurotis Pond

Hells Bay Canoe Trail

11

Alligator Creek

Long Lake

The Lung

12

West Lake Canoe Trail

Snake Bight Trail

13

Snake Bight

Mrazek Pond

Coot Bay Pond

14

15 Rowdy Bend Trail

16 Christian Point Trail

Wilderness Waterway

Mud Lake Canoe Trail

Flamingo

Flamingo Visitor Center

19-22

17 Eco Pond Loop

18 Coastal Prairie Trail

CAPE SABLE

N

10 mi.
10 km.

0
0

The Robert Is Here fruit stand, at the corner of Palm Drive and SW 192nd Avenue, is an iconic refreshment stop where visitors can purchase fresh local produce and enjoy an array of delicious tropical milk shakes. On your way to Everglades National Park, you will also pass agricultural fields, a mainstay of the local economy. Standard winter vegetables such as okra, tomatoes, sweet corn, squash, and beans are cultivated, but due to an influx of people from tropical regions around the world, you may also see such tropical crops as bananas, boniato, cassava, malanga, papaya, and dragon fruit. Tropical tree crops include avocado, carambola, longan, lychee, mamey sapote, and mango.

Ernest F. Coe Visitor Center

The Ernest F. Coe Visitor Center should be your first orientation stop at the main entrance to Everglades National Park. The daily hours of operation are 8 a.m. to 5 p.m. from mid-December through mid-April. Summer hours are 9 a.m. to 5 p.m. A good visitor center should beckon you to go explore the outdoors and this center does just that. Here you will find opportunities to learn about the Everglades through static and interactive interpretive displays, through educational videos, and from park rangers and volunteers at the front desk. A free brochure map of the park is available in English, Spanish, French, Italian, or German. Other

The Ernest Coe Visitor Center at the main entrance to Everglades National Park welcomes more than one million visitors a year.

Ernest F. Coe

No other person was more dedicated to making Everglades National Park a reality than Ernest F. Coe (1866–1951). He and other staunch environmentalists of the time, including author Marjory Stoneman Douglas (1890–1998), worked tirelessly to help save what was called "a worthless swamp" by developers. Their efforts were rewarded in December 1947 when President Harry S. Truman (1884–1972) dedicated the park in front of 10,000 onlookers. Ernest Coe was reluctantly sitting next to the president after being persuaded into attending the event by friends and colleagues.

His reluctance to attend the ceremony stemmed from the park's boundaries being drastically reduced in size from what he had envisioned. Coe wanted the park to encompass the area from the southern edge of Lake Okeechobee, not only to include the Big Cypress Swamp but the Upper Florida Keys as well. The boundaries agreed upon by politicians angered Coe, and he threatened to boycott the dedication. In retrospect, had Ernest Coe's vision become reality, the Everglades system would not be in the trouble it is today. By not including the area between the Big Cypress Swamp and Lake Okeechobee, politicians allowed what has been likened to owning the garden hose but not the faucet. Supported by import tariffs, Big Sugar, a controversial and politically powerful industry that cultivates thousands of acres of sugarcane in the rich muck south of Lake Okeechobee, has negatively altered the quantity and quality of water that reaches the Everglades. And this is one of the principal reasons why Everglades National Park became one of the most endangered parks in the nation. Without water there can be no Everglades.

Ernest F. Coe was, indeed, a true visionary. In addition to being recognized as a national treasure, Everglades National Park is also a designated World Heritage Site, an International Biosphere Reserve, and a Ramsar Wetland of International Importance.

informational handouts in various languages are also available upon request. For adventurous travelers who want to get off the beaten path, there is a free map called Hiking and Biking Trails of Long Pine Key available by request at the front desk and at the entrance station. This map shows all of the old fire roads that traverse Long Pine Key—these trails are excellent for hiking, and some are available for biking as well.

There is also a well-stocked bookstore and gift shop inside the Ernest F. Coe Visitor Center that offers many fine field guides and other educational books on the Everglades and surrounding areas. Look for other FalconGuides there. Guided walks, canoe trips, and boat tours are available in some areas of the park. Daily schedules can be obtained at the Ernest F. Coe Visitor Center, Royal Palm Visitor Center, or Flamingo Visitor Center, all accessible from the main entrance.

As a precaution against theft, be certain to lock all of your valuables in the trunk of your vehicle, not only at the Ernest F. Coe Visitor but anywhere that you stop and leave your vehicle.

User Fees

As you leave the Ernest F. Coe Visitor Center, the entrance station straddles the main park road and this is where various user fees are charged. As of this writing there is a proposed fee increase as part of the 2014–15 National Park Service review. Most of the revenue collected goes toward maintenance needs on infrastructure throughout the park. It is money well spent for those who enjoy the park's resources. Fees are charged for the following:

Vehicle Entrance
Pedestrian/Cyclist
Motorcycle
Annual Pass
RV w/Hookups
Front Country Camping
Backcountry Camping
Boating Permit 7-day
Boating Permit
Canoe/Kayak Permit

Seniors receive discounts on some fees. To check on current fees, please phone the Everglades National Park main office at (305) 242-7700, check the Everglades National Park website (nps.gov/ever), or inquire in person at any visitor center or entrance station.

The main entrance to Everglades National Park is open 24 hours a day, 365 days a year, except for closures due to hurricanes or other unforeseen circumstances.

Permitted Activities

Hiking, biking, boating, canoeing, kayaking, windsurfing, paddleboarding, camping, fishing, and photography are all permitted recreational activities within Everglades National Park. Camping and fishing are restricted to specified areas within the park. Check at the ranger stations for details regarding camping and fishing opportunities. Off-trail hiking (but not biking) is also allowed, but use your common sense. Take a manual compass or handheld GPS (Global Positioning System) to avoid getting lost, and learn which hazards you might encounter (poisonous plants, venomous snakes, dangerous animals). Large groups should practice environmental ethics and remain on designated trails to avoid creating trampled areas in pristine natural areas. An educational and safe way to enjoy off-trail exploring is to join one of the ranger-guided walks, some of which include wading into cypress domes and other wetland habitats. Ranger-guided canoe and bicycle trips are also available for a fee.

Concealed weapons are allowed if the owner holds a valid Concealed Weapon License, but discharging firearms inside the park is strictly forbidden. If you carry a concealed weapon and are not a Florida resident, be certain to check the list of Florida's reciprocity states to ensure you are legally allowed to possess a concealed firearm in Florida. You can check your legal status by visiting the Florida Department of Agriculture and Consumer Services website at freshfromflorida.com.

Prohibited and Restricted Activities

Personal watercraft (also called "Jet Skis" or "wet bikes"), waterskiing, airboats, all-terrain vehicles (ATVs), off-trail biking, remote-controlled drones, spearfishing, gigging, gill-netting, commercial fishing, and hunting are all prohibited within Everglades National Park. Airboat rides are currently available from private commercial enterprises located east of the main park entrance in Florida City and along Tamiami Trail (US 41). Rather than airboats, a more educational and relaxing way to enjoy the Everglades region is by foot, bicycle, or paddle.

Dogs are prohibited along trails but are allowed in parking lots and campgrounds if they are restrained on a leash (never allow a dog to approach areas where alligators reside). Guide dogs for visually impaired visitors are allowed on all trails. Horses are currently allowed along designated trails of Long Pine Key. Smoking is prohibited on all trails.

Be especially aware that feeding wildlife, especially alligators, is prohibited and can result in a fine.

Florida-panther-crossing signs are posted wherever this federal endangered cat is known to cross roadways. Slow down and remain alert when you see these signs, especially at night.

If alligators become accustomed to a food source, they will purposely approach people for handouts. This is not only a safety risk to you, because adult alligators do attack and sometimes kill people (and dogs), but also because once an alligator begins to habitually approach people for food, it is trapped and killed. Therefore, by illegally feeding an alligator, you create a threat to people and to the well-being of the alligator.

Campfires are allowed only below the high-tide line on specified beaches (prohibited at all other campsites, including land-based sites). Portable motors (generators, chain saws) are prohibited at all wilderness campsites.

Collecting plants, including air plants that have fallen to the ground, is prohibited. Parks and preserves harbor extremely rare plants, so removing even a single plant or picking a flower can be detrimental to a population. Admire their beauty and leave them where you found them, both for the benefit of the plant and for future explorers like yourself.

The playing of recorded birdcalls within the park is not allowed. Birders sometimes play recordings of calls to help bring birds into view for observation. This sometimes works too well, as demonstrated by a man who played a taped call of a barred owl along the Mahogany Hammock boardwalk in Everglades National Park. A resident barred owl in the hammock took offense at the "intruder owl" in its territory and attacked the man holding the recorder, leaving deep talon wounds in his face.

Also, do not exceed posted speed limits, both for your safety and for the benefit of wildlife in the park, and please brake for snakes, turtles, or other wildlife crossing the road. Panther-crossing signs are posted in areas where Florida panthers are known to cross roadways. This imperiled cat suffers more from road kills than any other threat (thirty were killed by vehicles in 2014). Law-enforcement rangers are in vehicles equipped with radar and they often monitor the speed of vehicles throughout the park. Slow down, relax, and enjoy the scenery.

Closed Areas

Closed areas represent less than 1 percent of the total area of Everglades National Park. Some areas may be temporarily closed in the event of fire, whether it is a wildfire or a prescribed burn being conducted by resource managers.

As of December 1, 2013, the Chekika Day Use Area is closed indefinitely until sufficient staff resources are available to maintain operations there. Check at the Ernest F. Coe Visitor Center or phone (305) 242-7700 for the current status.

There is one portion of northeast Florida Bay that is permanently closed because it is considered to be critical nesting habitat for the American crocodile. This area begins about 17 miles east of Flamingo and includes Little Madeira Bay, Taylor River, East Creek, Mud Creek, Mud Bay, Davis Creek, Joe Bay, Snag Bay, and the interior bays from the northern shore of Long Sound to US 1. The area is clearly posted with signage so do not enter this area for any reason. It is marked in color on the free Everglades National Park brochure map available at visitor centers and ranger stations.

Most keys and beaches in Florida Bay are closed to the public, with the exception of designated campsites on Little Rabbit Key and North Nest Key. Carl Ross Key, 6 miles south of Cape Sable and 9 miles southwest of Flamingo, was cut in half by Hurricane Wilma in 2005 and has since been closed to camping. It is now available only for day use with seasonal closures from October 15 to April 15 each year.

For a detailed listing of closed areas for boaters, consult the free Everglades Boating Regulations pamphlet available at all visitor centers and ranger stations.

The entire park may be closed to all entry during a hurricane. Campers, visitors, and boaters throughout the park may be ordered to vacate if a hurricane is imminent. Visitors in South Florida during the summer and fall should pay close attention to daily weather reports. A Hurricane Watch is issued if hurricane-force winds (74-plus mph) are expected within the next 36 hours, and a Hurricane Warning goes into effect if the storm can make landfall within 24 hours. Ample warning is given, so it is highly recommended that you evacuate South Florida if a hurricane is approaching. Hurricane Andrew devastated South Florida with 165-mph sustained winds (gusting to more than 200 mph) on August 24, 1992, and Hurricane Wilma struck Florida's southwest coast in October 2005. Its winds and storm surges ravaged Flamingo in Everglades National Park and caused so much destruction to the motel and cabins that they had to be removed. These facilities have yet to be replaced as of this writing.

Campgrounds

Campgrounds are available within Everglades National Park at Long Pine Key and Flamingo. The Flamingo campground is near the Flamingo Marina, which offers a visitor center, small restaurant, marina store, canoe and kayak rentals, restrooms, showers, and boat tours.

Boat Ramps

Boat ramps within Everglades National Park are located at Flamingo and West Lake. Watercraft with outboard motors of 6 horsepower or less are allowed in West Lake but not beyond. Commercial ramps are also available in Everglades City and on Chokoloskee Island on the west coast. Canoes, kayaks, and paddleboards can be launched from shorelines, including along the Flamingo campground. The launch area at Paurotis Pond is closed to paddlers during wading-bird nesting season. There is also a launch area at Coot Bay Pond (paddlers only) that accesses Coot Bay and the Everglades backcountry.

Burmese Pythons

Burmese pythons are native to Southeast Asia but have managed to colonize the Everglades and fully demonstrate their success at adaptability as a result of accidental escapes, irresponsible pet owners purposely releasing them, and hurricanes destroying enclosures of commercial suppliers. They have quickly become a very serious and daunting environmental concern by preying on native wildlife, including birds, mammals, and even American alligators. A single large Burmese python in a wading-bird rookery could be devastating as it feeds on eggs, hatchlings, and even adult birds.

Eggs of Burmese pythons might be eaten by raccoons, ants, or egg-eating native snakes, and juvenile pythons can fall prey to alligators, raccoons, bobcats, Florida panthers, hawks, herons, wood storks, large king snakes, and eastern indigo snakes. But once Burmese pythons become adults, they have very few predators in Florida. By 2003 researchers estimated the population of Burmese pythons within Everglades National Park to be well into the tens of thousands. Although two back-to-back severe freezes helped reduce their numbers considerably, warm winters since then have allowed them to rebound.

Burmese pythons are one of the world's largest snakes, and adults found in Florida have exceeded 17 feet in length. They average between 6 and 10 feet long. Although they are not venomous, they can inflict painful bites that may require medical attention, and full-grown Burmese pythons have killed young children in Florida.

If you come across a Burmese python in Everglades National Park, immediately phone the 24-hour dispatch at (305) 242-7740 and report the location. Do not attempt to capture or kill it. If you explore in Florida frequently, consider downloading a free app from iTunes called Ivegot1. This app allows you to forward photos and GPS locations to the Florida Fish and Wildlife Conservation Commission directly from your cell phone. You can also report sightings of any nonnative animal in Florida by phoning (888) IVE-GOT-1 (888-483-4681).

Burmese pythons are tan in color with irregular dark-brown blotches outlined in black. They have become a serious threat to wildlife in the Everglades and are most likely here to stay.

Motor Restrictions

Some areas within Everglades National Park are accessible only by canoe or kayak. For a complete listing of these areas, refer to the free Everglades Boating Regulations pamphlet, available at any visitor center or ranger station. Portions of the Hells Bay region are off-limits to powerboats, and some areas of Florida Bay are now Pole & Troll Zones, where powerboaters must tilt their motor up and either pole or use trolling motors. These areas are posted with signage. Boaters entering Seven Palm Lake must remove the motor from the transom. All areas beyond West Lake are no-motor zones.

Fishing Regulations

Be sure to pick up a copy of the free Everglades Fishing Regulations pamphlet from any visitor center or ranger station if you plan to try your luck fishing within Everglades National Park. This pamphlet is a supplement to the Florida Saltwater Recreational Fishing Regulations set by the state. Fishing regulations within Everglades National Park are sometimes stricter than state regulations, especially regarding possession limits, so make absolutely certain that you are fully informed before wetting a line. State regulations change occasionally, so stay up-to-date with the current size limits, possession limits, and seasonal closures.

Anglers may purchase licenses using a credit card by phoning (888) FISH-FLORIDA (888-347-4356) toll-free, or online at myfwc.org. Short-term visitor licenses are also available. The county tax collector's office, sporting-goods stores, bait-and-tackle shops, and other retail outlets that sell hunting and fishing equipment also sell licenses. For detailed information on fishing-license requirements and Florida fishing regulations, visit the Florida Fish and Wildlife Conservation Commission website (myfwc.org).

Professional fishing guides offer personalized guided fishing trips into Everglades National Park, and the half-day or full-day charter fee often includes a temporary fishing license for out-of-state visitors. For information on fishing-guide services in Florida, visit FLFishingCharters.com or inquire at the Flamingo Visitor Center or Gulf Coast Visitor Center in Everglades National Park. Motorized skiffs are also available for rent by private concessionaires at Flamingo and Everglades City.

A lone kayak fisherman heads out from the Flamingo campground into a blazing sunrise over Florida Bay.

Paddling the Everglades Backcountry and Frontcountry

Paddlers can enjoy hours—even days or weeks—exploring the backcountry waters of Everglades National Park. The 99-mile Everglades Wilderness Waterway (see Trail 22 in this guide), which connects Everglades City at the northwest corner of the park to Flamingo along Florida Bay to the south, is one of the last real wilderness adventures left in Florida (see Appendix F: Everglades National Park Campsite Information). All or any part of the Wilderness Waterway can be a rewarding, sometimes challenging experience for anyone who enjoys real wilderness adventure in a canoe or kayak. But use common sense and never embark on trips that may be beyond your physical abilities or skills. There are many enjoyable and less-challenging paddling excursions in Everglades National Park. To keep any boating adventure safe and enjoyable, see Appendix B: Paddling Safety Tips and Appendix C: Paddling Comfort Tips.

The front country of Flamingo offers something for everyone, whether it's a leisurely paddle in a rental canoe or kayak into Florida Bay to look at birds at low tide, a paddling excursion over Snake Bight or around the offshore islands to try your luck fishing, or fishing farther from Flamingo in a flats skiff. In short, let Flamingo be the beginning, not the end, of your Everglades experience. There are also two new chickees in Florida Bay available to paddlers and boaters for overnight camping.

Royal Palm Hammock

The turnoff to Royal Palm Hammock is a little more than a mile from the entrance station and is marked with signage. On your way to the Royal Palm Hammock turnoff, you may want to stop at the Taylor Slough Bridge to see what sort of wildlife and wildflowers are present. In October and November an interesting native terrestrial orchid, the fragrant ladies' tresses (*Spiranthes odorata*), blooms right along the edge of the road swale near the Taylor Slough Bridge. The attractive white flowers line an erect stem that often emerges from standing water, so expect to get your feet wet if you want a whiff of the sweet fragrance. Also look for alligators, fish, frogs, snakes, turtles, and wading birds in and around the deeper channel beneath the bridge and around culverts. Watch for common yellowthroats, red-winged blackbirds, limpkins, American bitterns, and occasional night-herons in the willow thickets near the bridge.

Royal Palm Hammock is located a couple of miles south of the main park road. Ranger-guided walks and talks are held here and the schedule is posted outside the Royal Palm Visitor Center. The visitor center includes a small bookstore, educational kiosks, restrooms, and vending machines. A seating area is available on the south side of the visitor center, where park rangers conduct interpretive programs.

Royal Palm Hammock gets its name from the royal palm (*Roystonea regia*), a tall, majestic palm that is native to South Florida. Early explorers and botanists used these towering palms as landmarks to find Royal Palm Hammock long before there were trails or roads leading into the Everglades.

There are three trails accessible from this location: Anhinga Trail, Gumbo Limbo Trail, and Old Ingraham Trail. This area was once the location of Royal Palm State Park, dedicated on November 22, 1916, and incorporated into Everglades National Park in 1947.

The trees in the parking-lot island are the native West Indian mahogany (*Swietenia mahagoni*), and you may notice their woody, brown fruits, which split open and release winged seeds that spiral in the air. You should be able to find parts of split fruits on the ground beneath the trees. Look for warblers in their canopy anytime from fall into spring. A native bromeliad called Spanish moss (*Tillandsia usneoides*) drapes from the branches like long, gray beards. Look closely for its tiny, green, fragrant flowers in late spring and summer.

Anhinga Trail offers visitors a chance to view a wide variety of wildlife from an elevated boardwalk that traverses a freshwater marsh. Bring your binoculars and camera.

Author's note: For unknown reasons, black vultures have acquired the habit of pulling rubber seals off car doors and tearing the rubber off windshield wipers. Plastic tarps and bungee cords are available at the Royal Palm Visitor Center to cover your vehicle and it is advised that you use them. To avoid the vultures, some visitors choose to park down the road and walk to the trail.

1 Anhinga Trail

See map on page 20.
Trailhead GPS coordinates: N25 22' 57.36" / W80 36' 34.61"
Type of trail: Walking
Type of adventure: Walk on a paved walkway and elevated boardwalk over a freshwater marsh (Taylor Slough).
Total distance: 0.75 mile
Difficulty: Easy. Wheelchair accessible.
Time required: 1 to 2 hours or more
Special considerations: Alligators sometimes rest very close to (or even on) the trail, so keep a safe distance even if they appear to be docile. For safety do not allow children to stand on the low barrier wall or the wood railing along the trail. Even in summer mosquitoes are usually tolerable along this trail during the daytime.
Scenic value: Excellent. This is an Everglades freshwater marsh with opportunities to observe resident and seasonal birds, reptiles, amphibians, fish, and diverse freshwater wetland plants. If you are looking for alligators, this is the place, especially in the dry season.

Overview and Route Description

The trailhead is located next to the visitor center. This is one of the most popular trails in all of Everglades National Park, so bring your camera, binoculars, and field guides. This is also where visitors often get their very first look at an American alligator in its natural habitat, and it is a very popular birding destination as well. Winter and spring are the best seasons to see an abundance of wildlife because lower water levels cause fish to concentrate in permanently flooded areas like Taylor Slough. The fish, in turn, attract birds, alligators, river otters, and other animals that come to feast on the bounty. There is usually an abundance of birds along the trail, and most can be viewed and photographed at close range because they are accustomed to pedestrians.

Double-crested cormorants, black vultures, and the trademark anhingas often perch on the low fence adjacent to the trail, allowing viewing at just a few feet away. Wood storks, herons, egrets, and moorhens are common sights. Anhingas nest in trees around the boardwalk, and their nesting activities can be seen from January into early summer. You may see

A female anhinga sits on eggs in her nest along Anhinga Trail. Anhingas begin nesting in January, and both parents tend to the eggs and young.

alligators positioned beneath the nests as they wait for a hapless nestling to fall. Young anhingas are white and fluffy with pinkish feet, unlike either of their parents. Green herons and other birds also nest here.

Specialty birds to look for here include purple gallinules, glossy ibis, wood storks, limpkins, and American bitterns. Short-tailed hawks, Swainson's hawks, red-tailed hawks, swallow-tailed kites, and even bald eagles sometimes soar overhead with groups of vultures. Red-shouldered hawks are resident and can be seen any time of year. Turtles and water snakes also can be seen around Taylor Slough. Unfortunately, a menagerie of exotic (nonnative) fish can be seen here, including walking catfish, blue tilapia, Mayan cichlids, and oscars, which now share the Everglades with such native fish as largemouth bass, bluegill, spotted gar, flagfish, topminnows, and mosquito fish.

Listen for the deep, throaty grunts of pig frogs in spring and summer. The low-pitched, guttural call of the male is given in a series—*grunt-grunt-grunt*—and the number of grunts in a series is based upon temperature, with more in warm, humid times of year. Listen also for the eerie, primal growling of mature alligators as nesting season approaches in early spring. The vibration created by a growling alligator causes the water over its back to ricochet up and down. When spring and summer rains begin, a melodious chorus of frogs can erupt all at once, especially at dusk. Common species include the southern chorus frog, green tree frog, southern cricket frog, spring peeper, little grass frog, southern leopard frog, and the ever-present pig frog. Standing out among the chorus you may also hear the sheeplike bleats of narrow-mouthed toads. If the mosquitoes aren't too bad, hang around after dark for the symphony. As nighttime approaches you may even hear the mournful cry of limpkins, which has been described as one of the eeriest sounds of nature, reminiscent of a wailing child.

Some of the flowering native plants that are easily visible along this trail include string-lily (*Crinum americanum*), floating hearts (*Nymphoides aquatica*), spatterdock (*Nuphar advena*), white water lily (*Nymphaea odorata*), ocean-blue morning-glory (*Ipomoea indica*), buttonbush (*Cephalanthus occidentalis*), arrowhead (*Sagittaria lancifolia*), butterfly orchid (*Encyclia tampensis*), cardinal air plant (*Tillandsia fasciculata*), and pickerelweed (*Pontederia cordata*). Trees and shrubs around the boardwalk include pond apple (*Annona glabra*), buttonbush (*Cephalanthus occidentalis*), cocoplum (*Chrysobalanus icaco*), strangler fig (*Ficus aurea*), and red bay (*Persea borbonia*). The tall grass surrounding much of the trail is common reed (*Phragmites australis*). Take your time and enjoy the show of nature along this trail. It sure beats Disney World!

2 Gumbo Limbo Trail

See map on page 20.
Trailhead GPS coordinates: N25 22' 55.40" / W80 36' 34.46"
Type of trail: Walking
Type of adventure: Short walk on a paved trail through Royal Palm Hammock
Total distance: 0.5 mile
Difficulty: Easy. Wheelchair accessible.
Time required: Half an hour
Special considerations: Mosquitoes and biting flies in summer and fall
Scenic value: Good. This is a mature tropical hardwood hammock with numerous species of native tropical trees and associated birds and other wildlife.

Overview and Route Description

The trailhead is located on the south side of the visitor center. About 85 percent of the trees in the hammocks of Everglades National Park are of tropical origin, and this trail is named for the gumbo-limbo (*Bursera simaruba*), a tropical tree characterized by thin, peeling, red bark. The gumbo-limbo trees are easily recognized along the trail. This is also an excellent trail to look for warblers and other birds during fall and spring migration. Keep an eye and ear out for vireos, flycatchers, gnatcatchers, cuckoos, and other resident or migratory birds that inhabit hardwood forests. Barred owls can sometimes be seen in this and other hammocks throughout the park and their loud calls can be heard most any time of day but especially at dusk. Here you can also see some interesting epiphytes—ferns, orchids, and bromeliads—by closely examining the trunks and branches of trees, especially rough-barked species such as live oak (*Quercus virginiana*). Look on smooth-barked trees for colorful, endangered liguus tree snails (*Liguus fasciatus*). Do not disturb the snails, and especially do not remove them from the trees when they are dormant during the dry season because they will not be able to survive. If you think you hear crickets, you are most likely hearing the calls of the greenhouse frog (*Eleutherodactylus planirostris*) hiding amid the leaf litter on the forest floor. This small, brown frog is native to the West Indies but is established throughout much of Florida.

ABOUT THE GUMBO-LIMBO

The gumbo-limbo (*Bursera simaruba*) is one of the most interesting trees of the Everglades. Any piece of a trunk or branch will root if placed in the ground, giving rise to the name "living fencepost" in parts of its native range. Even when a gumbo-limbo is toppled by storm winds, the roots that face upward simply sprout leaves and grow into trees. The thin bark allows the tree to photosynthesize through the trunk and branches in the dappled light of hammocks, and this trait is especially useful when the tree is leafless in late winter and spring. Now-extinct Calusa Indians in southwestern Florida once used the sap of this tree as a source of birdlime. Birdlime is sticky tree sap smeared on branches to entrap birds that land on it. The Calusa trapped native songbirds in this manner, then put them in makeshift cages and transported them in oceangoing canoes carved from cypress trunks (some up to 40 feet long) to Cuba to trade for tobacco and other goods.

When African slaves were brought to Florida decades later, some of them learned of the use of the gumbo-limbo as a source of birdlime and used the sap to trap birds for food and trade. Some of these Africans were from the Bantu tribe, who were adept at using birdlime in their homeland. The Bantu name for the tree became nkômbô edimbu (translating to "runaway slave's birdlime"), and the name was modified in English as "gumbo-limbo" over time.

Early settlers even used the straight trunks of young gumbo-limbo trees to pen West Indian manatees. The wood is light and floats in seawater so bundles of the trunks could be floated into the shallows and shoved into the soft mud of Florida Bay to make large corrals. West Indian manatees, or "sea cows," were kept penned as a source of food, much like cattle. Today these areas are still indicated on nautical charts as the Cow Pens.

The sap of the gumbo-limbo also has been used as an ingredient in varnish; the wood has been carved into merry-go-round horses; and the fruits are a favorite food of flycatchers (especially kingbirds) in southern Florida. The comical name "tourist tree" relates to the red peeling bark that resembles the skin of sunburned tourists. Other names are gum-elemi and West Indian birch. It is closely related to two other trees with aromatic resin, frankincense and myrrh.

The gumbo-limbo has a long history of uses in Florida by Native Americans, African slaves, and early settlers.

3 Old Ingraham Trail

Trailhead GPS coordinates: N25 22' 55.84" / W80 36' 36.05"
Type of trail: Hiking, backpacking, and tent camping
Type of adventure: Hike or backpack on an unpaved historic roadway.
Total distance: 22.0 miles from Royal Palm Hammock and back
Difficulty: Moderate
Time required: All-day round-trip hike. Two campsites are available by permit for backpackers along the trail if you do not want to make the round-trip in a single day.
Special considerations: Mosquitoes and biting flies in summer and fall. Large alligators sometimes bask on the trail. No facilities.
Scenic value: Excellent. The trail traverses a variety of habitats with occasional open vistas of the Everglades.

Overview and Route Description

Historic Old Ingraham Trail can be accessed off Gumbo Limbo Trail or at the southwest corner of the cleared area near the parking lot of Royal Palm Hammock. It was once the road that led to Flamingo but was closed after the new road was completed. Old Ingraham Trail is not marked with

Two sibling raccoon babies stare from a tree along Old Ingraham Trail.

Old Ingraham Trail

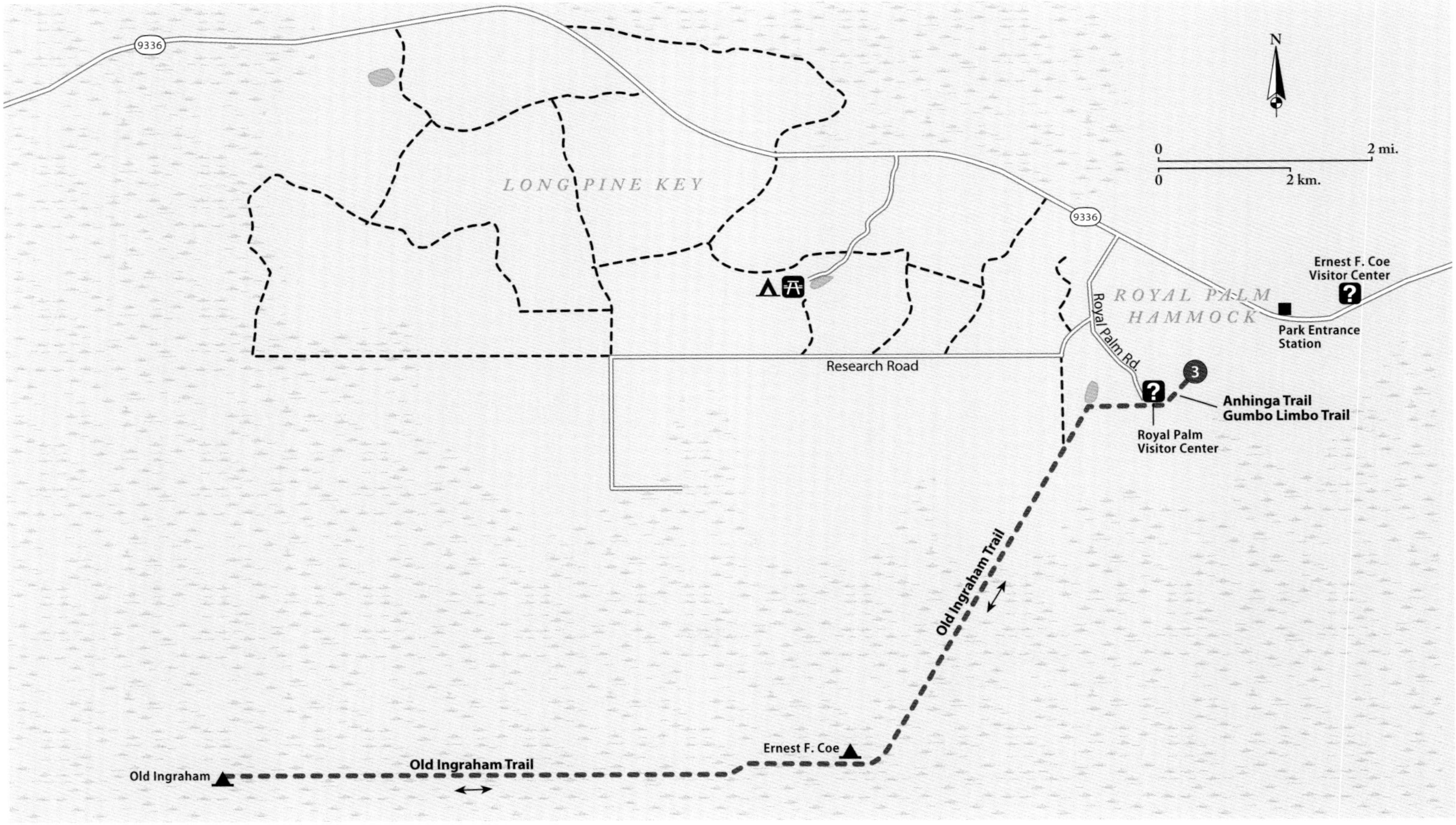

N

2 mi.

2 km.

0   0

Ernest F. Coe
Visitor Center

ROYAL PALM
HAMMOCK

Park Entrance
Station

9336

Royal Palm Rd.

**Anhinga Trail
Gumbo Limbo Trail**

Royal Palm
Visitor Center

Old Ingraham Trail

Research Road

LONGPINE KEY

Ernest F. Coe

Old Ingraham Trail

Old Ingraham

signage, but it offers good birding opportunities as it bisects various habitats. It is a wide trail that is excellent for hikers and backpackers. Because the trail is seldom traveled, it is especially nice for those seeking solitude.

Back when this area was a part of Royal Palm State Park, a local Women's Garden Club planted exotic bromeliads, ferns, and other plants near the entrance to Old Ingraham Trail to help beautify the area. Even residents in South Florida at the time regarded the Everglades as rather boring, so the consensus was that exotic plants were necessary to make the area more interesting and colorful for visiting tourists. Tucked away just off the trail is an old limestone pavilion where dried corn was used to attract deer for viewing by tourists.

Old Ingraham Trail runs south-southwest for about 6 miles and then turns due west. The Ernest F. Coe campsite is 6 miles from the trailhead at Royal Palm Hammock, and the Old Ingraham campsite is at the end of the 11-mile trail. A required backcountry camping permit can be obtained at the main entrance station. Readers should note that the entire Old Ingraham Trail just recently received official wilderness designation, meaning bicycling is no longer allowed.

Research Road—Hole-in-the-Donut

Midway between the main park road and Royal Palm Hammock is a paved road that leads west to the Daniel Beard Research Center and to an area of fallow agricultural land called the Hole-in-the-Donut. The agricultural land was abandoned in the 1970s after the National Park Service deemed it to be inappropriate for the continuation of commercial agriculture within the park boundaries. The area quickly became overgrown with exotic pest plants, mostly Brazilian pepper (*Schinus terebinthifolius*), a large aggressive shrub from South America, and shoebutton ardisia (*Ardisia elliptica*), an invasive shrub from tropical Asia. These two species formed a near monoculture across hundreds of acres.

In order to reclaim the disturbed land, an ambitious project was implemented to clear away the exotic vegetation and then scrape it down below grade to allow flooding in the rainy season. Native freshwater wetland plants moved in and the area is now recovering. It has quickly become one of the best places to see white-tailed deer, waterfowl, and other resident and seasonal wildlife. Most of the accumulated fill that resulted from scraping the area was used to create large elevated pads that offer refuge for small herds of white-tailed deer, so it is always a good idea to scan the area with binoculars or spotting scopes.

This road turns south just past the Daniel Beard Research Center but a new pipe gate blocks further vehicle travel. You can either hike or bicycle from here. The road terminates at an abandoned missile site established during the Cuban missile crisis. The Soviet Union was placing missiles in Cuba, just 90 miles from the United States, so President John F. Kennedy placed a military ship blockade around Cuba, which created a standoff. The Soviet Union ended up removing the missile bases from Cuba and avoided a potential nuclear war.

Everglades National Park now offers special guided tours of this Cold War–relic missile site for park visitors. Check the Ernest F. Coe Visitor or the Royal Palm Visitor Center for tour schedules or look for a sign advertising the tours at the Research Road intersection.

Long Pine Key

As you continue west on the main park road, Long Pine Key is the next turnoff past Royal Palm Hammock. Long Pine Key is the principal upland area of Everglades National Park and encompasses nearly 20,000 acres of pine rockland habitat interspersed with more than 120 tropical hardwood hammocks. Long Pine Key is periodically bisected by wide swaths of Everglades prairie, often called finger glades, through which water flows during the wet season. The word *key* in Florida, and *cay* (pronounced key) in the Bahamas, originally came from *cairi*, a Lucayan word for "island." The Lucayans were an Arawak tribe from the Bahamas. This is also the origin of the Spanish *cayo*, which translates to "a small, low-lying island." This word aptly fits Long Pine Key, a low-lying island of pines and hammocks surrounded by glades that are flooded throughout most of the year.

The Long Pine Key turnoff leads to a campground, picnic area, and restrooms. It is also an access road to some outstanding hiking and biking trails. The campground can accommodate both recreational vehicles and tent campers. Campsites are only available on a first-come, first-served basis so in the unlikely event that this campground is full, you will need to continue on to the Flamingo campground. Signs will be posted at the entrance station and along the main park road at the Long Pine Key turnoff if the campground is full.

There is a lake bordering the campground and picnic area (swimming prohibited; fishing allowed) that was dredged for fill to create the main park road. Look for black-necked stilts and other shorebirds along the shoreline. On your way to the campground area on Long Pine Key, you will pass the Long Pine Key Nature Trail (see Trail 4). Look for eastern bluebirds and brown-headed nuthatches in the pinelands near the restrooms. Both of these birds were successfully reintroduced after being extirpated from the region, as were wild turkeys.

Long Pine Key in Everglades National Park is mostly covered by pine rockland, a habitat listed as globally imperiled by the State of Florida. Less than 2 percent of the historic coverage of pine rockland habitat in Miami-Dade County outside of Everglades National Park remains.

4 Long Pine Key Nature Trail (Gate 4 to Gate 8)

Trailhead GPS coordinates: N25 24' 12.65" / W80 39' 16.65"
Type of trail: Hiking or biking
Type of adventure: Bike or hike on a graded fire road that traverses pine rockland and prairie habitats, with opportunities to explore nearby hardwood hammocks.
Total distance: 12.5 miles round-trip (read the notes at the end of this trail description)
Charts: *Hiking and Biking Trails of Long Pine Key* available for free at the Ernest F. Coe Visitor Center; *National Geographic Trails Illustrated Map #243: Everglades National Park*
Difficulty: Moderate
Time required: A half to a full day
Special considerations: Mosquitoes and biting flies in summer and fall. Bring water and snacks if you plan on traveling the entire trail. Mountain or hybrid bikes are advised because rough, rocky areas occur whenever the trail crosses open prairie habitat. These same areas may be flooded during the rainy season with water up to 12 inches deep across the trail.
Scenic value: Outstanding. The trail traverses pristine upland and wetland habitats.

Overview and Route Description

This is one of the best trails in Everglades National Park but also one of the least used. The trail offers opportunities to explore pine rockland, prairie, and tropical hardwood hammock habitats. White-tailed deer can sometimes be seen on or near the trail, and this is also where a truly fortunate visitor might see a Florida panther. Look for animal tracks in muddy areas, especially where the trail cuts through prairie habitat. Tracks may include deer, raccoons, bobcats, Florida panthers, snakes, alligators, and wading birds. Tiny oak toads (*Bufo quercicus*) are common along the trail and are typically only ½ to 1 inch long. Explore the open prairies on foot to see an abundance of native wildflowers, but be cautious of venomous snakes, especially cottonmouth moccasins around low-lying areas with standing water.

Simpson's grass-pink (*Calopogon tuberosus* var. *simpsonii*) can be seen flowering in these prairies from April into June. The flowers of this

Long Pine Key Nature Trail (Gate 4 to Gate 8)

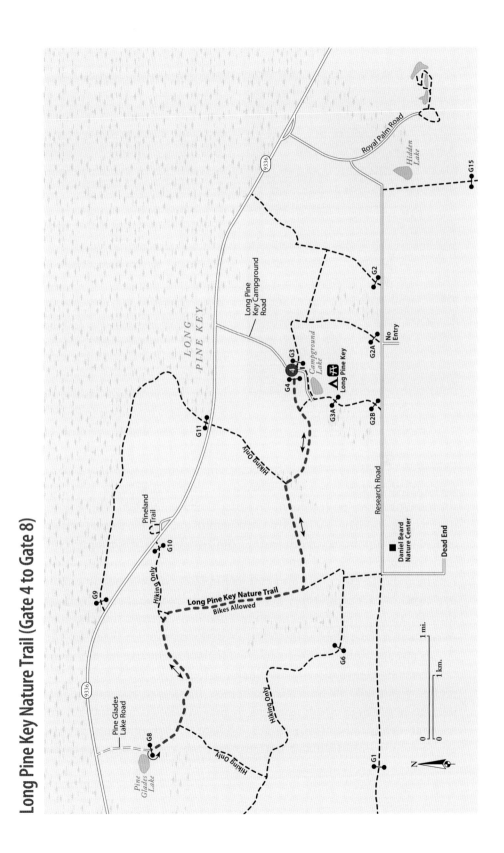

Simpson's grass-pink is a common terrestrial orchid found in the prairies of Long Pine Key. Look for it in springtime.

attractive native orchid range in color from rich rosy pink to nearly white and are produced on stems that stand above the surrounding grasses. It is often accompanied by another spring-flowering native orchid, the spring ladies' tresses (*Spiranthes vernalis*), with small white flowers that spiral up the stem.

Along with the common butterflies that can be found along this trail are two federal endangered rarities—the Florida leafwing and Bartram's scrub-hairstreak. The Florida leafwing is a fast-flying reddish-orange butterfly that closely resembles a leaf when it lands (the undersides of the wings are mottled grayish brown). Bartram's scrub-hairstreak is bluish gray with a few bold, white stripes and a bright-orange patch on the lower hind wing. If you are interested in butterflies, look for these two rare species along the Long Pine Key Nature Trail where it bisects pine rockland habitat. Keep a watchful eye out for the red-white-and-blue faithful beauty moth and the pink-winged rattlebox moth, both day-flying species.

The trail will eventually lead you to Pine Glades Lake near the main park road, a good rest stop for a picnic before heading back. From fall through spring there are sometimes thousands of tree swallows that swarm across the surface of this lake to get a sip of water on the wing. This is a spectacular sight if you're lucky enough to be at the lake for this event.

Also look for swallow-tailed kites soaring above the lake and surrounding pineland in spring and summer. These graceful birds of prey migrate north from South America to nest in Florida, and they're very adept at seeing and catching snakes and lizards. They also hunt for nests of other birds and will snatch nestlings even while being attacked by the parents. Witnessing this can be somewhat disheartening, but swallow-tailed kites have hungry young of their own to feed.

Although this can be a loop trail by returning to Gate 4 via the main park road, it is safer to return the same way you came. Be absolutely certain you stay on the same trail that you took to get to Pine Glades Lake because there are other turnoffs that can take you many miles in the wrong direction (and they are officially off-limits to bicycles). Consult the *Hiking and Biking Trails of Long Pine Key* map, or if you are a high-tech traveler, a handheld GPS will also keep you on the correct trail. The *National Geographic Trails Illustrated Map 243: Everglades National Park* is also very useful for these trails (this chart is available at visitor center bookstores in Everglades National Park or ordered through the National Geographic online catalog). The Long Pine Key Nature Trail (Gate 4 to Gate 8) is the only sanctioned bicycling trail on Long Pine Key. All others are open for hiking only.

Alternate route: A much shorter loop trail (hiking only) is available from Gate 4. Hike west on the trail about halfway across the first prairie and then follow the narrow but well-defined footpath that you will see on your left. This leads you through or around Mosier Hammock to the campground lake. Watch for eastern bluebirds in the vicinity of the restrooms and picnic areas. A pair of very rare western spindalis nested in this vicinity in the summer of 2009, marking the first documented nesting of this bird in the United States. This bird was once called the stripe-headed tanager and is found in the "Accidentals from the tropics" section of some field guides.

Pine Glades Lake

This scenic, man-made lake is accessible by vehicles from the main park road (SR 9336) by taking the second left turnoff about 2.9 miles past the Pineland Trail. The first left is a gated fire road (Gate 10) that leads to the Long Pine Key Nature Trail. The Pine Glades Lake turnoff is not signed, so visitors often miss it (look for the stop sign at the turnoff exit). This is a dirt road that may be partly flooded during the wet season, but the parking area next to the lake will be dry.

There is a narrow footpath that circles the lake and this can be a rewarding hike for wildflower enthusiasts. Pine Glades Lake was dredged for fill to build the main park road that leads to Flamingo. Fishing is allowed but swimming is prohibited. Because this lake is infrequently visited, it can be a nice, quiet place to picnic or to just sit and enjoy the scenery and solitude. This can also be a worthwhile stop for birders and it is one of the more scenic places within the park to watch the sunset. After sunset look for bats over the lake, sometimes flying low enough to sip water on the wing just like tree swallows do in daytime.

This is the terminus of the Long Pine Key Nature Trail (see Trail 4 in this guide) if you bypassed the Long Pine Key turnoff. If you enter this trail from Pine Glades Lake (Gate 8), the first quarter mile or so is rough and rocky so if you are bicycling, you may want to walk your bike through this section.

Tricolored herons are commonly seen around Pine Glades Lake and other freshwater areas, where they hunt small fish, snails, frogs, and juvenile snakes.

5 Mosier Hammock Trail

Mosier Hammock was named to honor the first warden of Royal Palm State Park, Charles A. Mosier (1871–1936). Royal Palm State Park was dedicated in 1916 but was incorporated into Everglades National Park in 1947. Charles Mosier has been further commemorated in the naming of long-stalked stopper (*Mosiera longipes*), Florida brickellbush (*Brickellia mosieri*), and a color form of liguus tree snail (*Liguus fasciatus mosieri*).

Trailhead GPS coordinates: N25 23' 59.17" / W80 39' 33.32"

Type of trail: Hiking

Type of adventure: Hike through a pristine tropical hardwood forest.

Total distance: 0.5-mile loop

Difficulty: Easy

Time required: Half an hour

Special considerations: Exposed tree roots and limestone on the trail. Mosquitoes and biting flies in summer and fall. Poison ivy and poisonwood occur along the trail.

Scenic value: Excellent. This is a scenic inside view of a tropical hardwood forest.

Overview and Route Description

The easiest way to access the Mosier Hammock Trail is to park in the last parking area past the turnoff to the Long Pine Key campground. Look for the trailhead on the north side of the parking area. This trail will lead you around the east side of Mosier Hammock. You will eventually see a side trail leading to the north, but keep to the left and the trail will loop around directly through Mosier Hammock. Inside the hammock look for endangered liguus tree snails (*Liguus fasciatus*) on the trunks of trees. The name *liguus* (pronounced LIG-you-us) means "banded," and these snails were what inspired the colorful patterns on garments made by Seminole and Miccosukee Indians. Many hammocks in the Everglades bear the names of tree snail collectors but collecting the shells of these colorful snails is now illegal. Mosier Hammock is also a good place to look for birds, especially during spring and fall migration.

Continue along the trail and it will eventually exit at the campground lake. Bear left at the lake and hike along the shoreline until you come to the campground road. Follow the road east back to your vehicle.

Mosier Hammock Trail

Colorful liguus tree snails can often be seen on trees along Mosier Hammock Trail. There are sixty color forms of this endangered snail in southern Florida and many more in Cuba.

Alternate route: If you would like this to be a longer loop, take the narrow footpath that leads north from the Mosier Hammock Trail across an Everglades prairie and, when you reach the Long Pine Key Nature Trail, turn right and this will take you back to Gate 4. Turn right at the road to return to the parking area and restrooms. You can also park your car at Gate 4 and hike west to the first open glade. Near the far western end of this glade is a narrow footpath leading south (left) that will lead you to the Mosier Hammock Trail. Turn right to hike through the hammock or bear left to circumnavigate the hammock. When you arrive at the road, you will have about a 10-minute walk back to your vehicle.

6 Pineland Trail

The Pineland Trail is 2 miles west of the Long Pine Key turnoff on the main park road (SR 9336). This is a short, paved loop that traverses pine rockland habitat. If you have already hiked or biked the Long Pine Key Nature Trail, you may wish to bypass the Pineland Trail because it will be somewhat repetitious. There are, however, a few wildflowers and other native plants that can be seen along this trail that you may have missed on other trails. If you have plenty of time, or if you haven't already hiked the fire road trails, this trail can be rewarding, both in the number of birds and butterflies and the number of flowering plants you may encounter. There are interpretive signs along the way, as well as a kiosk at the trailhead. Portable restrooms are sometimes available in the parking area.

See map on page 20.

Trailhead GPS coordinates: N25 25' 23.45" / W80 40' 46.47"

Type of trail: Walking

Type of adventure: Walk on a short, paved loop trail through pine rockland habitat.

Total distance: 0.5 mile

Difficulty: Easy. Wheelchair accessible.

Time required: Half an hour

Special considerations: Mosquitoes and biting flies in summer and fall

Scenic value: Good. Wildflowers can be abundant along this trail.

Overview and Route Description

Although this is a short, paved trail, it offers a good opportunity to see and photograph many interesting and rare flowering plants, especially for visitors who use wheelchairs or walkers. It is one of the few places in Everglades National Park where you can find Cuban nakedwood (*Colubrina cubensis* var. *floridana*). This rare, endangered shrub or small tree has oblong leaves that are softly hairy. The small, star-shaped, fragrant flowers are greenish yellow and produced in clusters. The name "nakedwood" refers to the shedding bark. An endemic morning-glory relative, pineland clustervine (*Jacquemontia curtisii*) is rather abundant along this trail. It is a petite vine with half-inch, starlike white flowers that glisten in the sunlight. Look for it climbing around on shrubs along the trail. In the cool winter months, also look for snakes lying on the warm asphalt of this trail. Remember, only lucky visitors get to see snakes in the Everglades!

The pineland clustervine is one of many wildflowers along the Pineland Trail. It is endemic to Florida and is a state-listed threatened species.

The dominant overstory tree in the pinelands of Everglades National Park is the slash pine (*Pinus elliottii*), so named because in order to harvest the sap to make varnish and other products, a V-shaped slash is made in the trunk and then a container is strapped to the tree just below the cuts to collect the oozing sap. The wood of slash pines growing in pine rocklands of Miami-Dade County is much denser than that of the same species growing throughout the rest of the southeastern United States. This is due to them growing very slowly on limestone, where there is little soil. Lumbermen coined the name "Dade County pine" for lumber harvested from slash pines growing in pine rocklands, which demanded a higher price because the wood was impervious to termites and aging. Many homes built of Dade County pine lumber in the early 1900s have stood the test of time.

7 Pa-Hay-Okee

The name *pahayokee* comes from the language of the Seminole and translates to "great grass water." Bring your camera because this elevated overlook gives you the opportunity to see, and better appreciate, the vastness of the region that famed author Marjory Stoneman Douglas called a "River of Grass."

See map on page 20.

Trailhead GPS coordinates: N25 26' 27.23" / W80 47' 01.16"

Type of trail: Elevated wood boardwalk leading to a sheltered overlook

Type of adventure: Walking

Total distance: 280 yards round-trip

Difficulty: Easy. Wheelchair accessible.

Time required: 20 minutes or more, depending on how long you wish to enjoy the scenery

Special considerations: None. There are stairs leading up the east (right) side of the overlook, and a wheelchair-accessible ramp is on the west (left) side. Mosquitoes are generally at tolerable levels even in summer.

Scenic value: Exceptional. This is one of the best scenic vistas and photo opportunities in Everglades National Park, especially at sunrise.

Overview and Route Description

The view to the north from the covered overlook encompasses the southern edge of the Shark River Slough. The slough is a broad expanse of Everglades prairie dotted with tree islands through which a vast sheet of water flows slowly from the Big Cypress Swamp into the maze of deep tidal rivers that empty into Whitewater Bay and the Gulf of Mexico. Seminole Indians once plied this shallow grassy river in dugout canoes, poling their way along without the aid of compasses or GPS units.

The headwaters of the Shark River Slough can be seen at Shark Valley in the northern Everglades off Tamiami Trail (US 41). Far to the west there is a broad expanse of mangroves that grow in the brackish water created by the freshwater of the Everglades mixing with the salt water of the Gulf of Mexico along Florida's coast. This biologically rich region serves as a critical nursery ground for countless fish, crustaceans, and other marine organisms. The trees themselves offer protected areas for wading-bird rookeries and nests of ospreys and bald eagles. So the water you see at the Pa-Hay-Okee overlook serves a vital purpose, not only as a

Pa-Hay-Okee offers a grand view of one of the most picturesque vistas in the Everglades, especially at sunrise.

critical component for the health of the interior Everglades, but also for the vast mangrove swamps and brackish estuaries of the coastal regions.

In late spring and summer, you may hear yellow-billed cuckoos calling from the tree islands near the overlook, as well as great crested flycatchers and other resident birds.

8 Mahogany Hammock

See map on page 20.
Trailhead GPS coordinates: N25 19' 24.93" / W80 49' 55.47"
Type of trail: Elevated wood boardwalk
Type of adventure: Walking
Total distance: 0.5 mile
Difficulty: Easy. Wheelchair accessible.
Time required: 30 minutes to 1 hour; birders could spend 2 hours or more
Special considerations: Mosquitoes and biting flies in summer and fall
Scenic value: Excellent. This elevated boardwalk provides a bird's-eye view of a tropical hardwood hammock surrounded by freshwater marsh.

Overview and Route Description

As its name implies, the West Indian mahogany (*Swietenia mahagoni*) can be found in this hammock. Mahogany Hammock is surrounded by freshwater marsh with a deeper moat adjacent to the hammock, created by water flow; both help spare the hammock from lightning fires that race across the surrounding prairies in the rainy season. The entire region can be bone dry in spring before the rainy wet season makes its annual debut. The national champion West Indian mahogany can be seen adjacent to the boardwalk, its ancient, weatherworn trunk and limbs showing signs of past lightning strikes and hurricanes.

The spreading root systems of huge fallen trees next to the boardwalk attest to the strength of Hurricane Andrew. This Category 5 storm, with gusting winds that exceeded 200 mph, passed directly over the Everglades on August 24, 1992.

Mahogany Hammock is a popular place for birders to look for warblers and other songbirds during spring and fall migration, and there are barred owls present year-round. Listen for their loud calls—which sound as if they are asking *who cooks for you, who cooks for you all?*—any time of day but especially at dusk. Barred owls nest in this hammock so keep an eye out for white, fluffy fledgling owls perched in trees near the

The Mahogany Hammock boardwalk invites visitors to explore the interior of a shady tropical hardwood hammock and is a good location to find barred owls.

boardwalk. In the expanses of saw-grass prairies surrounding Mahogany Hammock (and the next few miles past the hammock), you might see endangered Cape Sable seaside sparrows. They are most easily seen in springtime when males perch on the tall flowering spikes of saw grass while singing to potential mates with a series of clicks and trills. It is the only bird restricted entirely to the Everglades region.

Among the plants visible from the boardwalk are some interesting ferns, bromeliads, and both epiphytic and terrestrial native orchids. The large, robust leather fern (*Acrostichum danaeifolium*) is especially common, as is the long-leaved strap fern (*Campyloneurum phyllitidis*). On calm days you may detect a slight skunk-like odor emitted by a native tree called white stopper (*Eugenia axillaris*). The tree was once used medicinally to treat diarrhea, hence the name "stopper." Watch for poison ivy (*Toxicodendron radicans*) draping from trees along the boardwalk. You will see another woody vine with large, paired leaflets called medicine vine (*Hippocratea volubilis*), named to honor Hippocrates, who is often referred to as the father of western medicine. Medicine vine has been used medicinally for centuries.

Keep an eye out for eastern indigo snakes, yellow rat snakes, and Florida king snakes inside the hammock, or check for mangrove water snakes in the shallow water near the elevated boardwalk between the parking area and the hammock. There are three distinct color forms of the mangrove water snake: red, black, and tan. This is definitely a place to take your time and carefully scrutinize the hammock for plants and animals that the average visitor may pass by.

Paurotis Pond

Paurotis Pond is located along the main park road between Mahogany Hammock and Nine Mile Pond and is indicated by signage near the entrance. Canoeing and kayaking are allowed only during fall and winter, but it is a relatively small pond that is mostly used by anglers. It is off-limits during nesting season from spring through summer, and a sign is posted at a small surface ramp during times of closure. This is a worthwhile stop to view roseate spoonbills, wood storks, egrets, and herons roosting (year-round) and nesting (spring to early summer) in the trees surrounding this scenic pond. A spotting scope will help. There are a couple of picnic tables if you would like to have lunch or a snack. There are no restroom facilities.

A beautiful roseate spoonbill flies toward its roost at Paurotis Pond after feeding on the mud flats of Florida Bay.

9 Nine Mile Pond

It is said that the name Nine Mile Pond came about because it was 9 miles from an old ranger station near Flamingo, which would place it at the Rowdy Bend trailhead. Nine Mile Pond is marked with signage on the south side of the main park road with two entrances and exits to the parking area. When water levels are low, parts of the paddling trail can be impassable. This usually occurs late in the dry season from March to May. This can change from year to year depending on unseasonal rainfall. Even if you are not a canoeist or kayaker, this is still a worthwhile stop to look for wading birds, waterfowl, and alligators.

Trailhead GPS coordinates: N25 15' 14.00" / W80 47' 52.58"

Type of trail: Canoeing or kayaking

Type of adventure: Paddle along a marked trail through mangroves and an Everglades marsh.

Total distance: 5.5 miles to complete the entire loop

Charts: *National Geographic Trails Illustrated Map 243: Everglades National Park* has good detail of this trail in an inset.

Difficulty: Easy to moderate

Time required: 3 to 5 hours

Special considerations: Mosquitoes and biting flies in summer and fall. Be cautious of large alligators, especially if you are fishing. Paddleboards are not advised. Bring bottled water.

Scenic value: Excellent

Overview and Route Description

This scenic paddling trail winds through shallow freshwater marsh habitat studded with small tree islands, cattails, and red mangroves. Look for alligators and an array of resident and migratory birds along with other wildlife associated with freshwater marshes. The endangered snail kite can sometimes be seen here along with wood storks, white pelicans, roseate spoonbills, herons, egrets, ducks, gallinules, and an assortment of songbirds. You will also see paurotis palms (*Acoelorrhaphe wrightii*) growing along this trail in their natural habitat. This state-listed endangered species occurs only in Collier, Miami-Dade, and Monroe Counties in Florida and is so attractive that it is grown commercially for landscaping.

Nine Mile Pond

Nine Mile Pond is an easy trip for novice paddlers because it is a shallow loop trail marked with numbered posts, and the trail is mostly protected from wind. Canoes are available here to rent during the busy tourist season (late fall through spring), and park rangers also offer guided canoe trips at this location (additional fee). You will need to rent the canoes at the Flamingo concessionaire next to the marina store and then drive back. The canoe rental includes paddles and life vests.

There is a rather steep drop-off along sections of the shoreline where you launch, so test the depth with your paddle and be aware of large alligators. Once you have launched in Nine Mile Pond, paddle due east (straight across the pond) to Marker 1, where a creek cuts through a marl prairie. Follow the marked trail about 3 miles to Marker 44, where you will have a decision to make: You can either take a shortcut at this junction or complete the entire loop. To take the shortcut, turn northeast to Marker 44A and on to Marker 82 on the north side of the loop, and then turn left at Marker 82 to return to the parking area. To complete the full loop, turn southeast at Marker 44 and continue your journey.

On your way back, as you pass Marker 98 near journey's end, you will paddle across two small ponds just before you reach the main pond at the trailhead. Scan the edges of these two ponds for an enormous American crocodile. It likes to sun on the banks or hang out in the middle of the ponds. American crocodiles are not as dangerous to humans as are large alligators, so try to forget what you've read about Nile crocodiles in Africa or saltwater crocodiles in Australia attacking and killing people.

A large American crocodile resides in Nine Mile Pond, where it eats alligators, wading birds, waterfowl, fish, and turtles. They are not as dangerous to people as large American alligators.

10 Noble Hammock Canoe Trail

See map on page 20.

Trailhead GPS coordinates: Entrance: N25 14' 08.05" / W80 49' 04.26"

Type of trail: Canoe or kayak (motors prohibited)

Type of adventure: Paddle along a loop trail through mangroves and a tropical hardwood hammock.

Total distance: 2.0-mile loop. The exit point for the Noble Hammock Canoe Trail is about 140 yards west of the entrance so hike east (to your right) back to your vehicle.

Charts: *National Geographic Trails Illustrated Map #243: Everglades National Park*

Difficulty: Easy

Time required: 1 to 2 hours or more

Special considerations: Mosquitoes and biting flies in summer and fall. Some tight turns are difficult to navigate, especially for long sea kayaks.

Scenic value: Good. This trail meanders through mangroves and passes paurotis palms and a hardwood hammock on a shell mound where there was once an illegal moonshine operation.

Overview and Route Description

The Noble Hammock trailhead is marked with signage on the south side of the main park road between Nine Mile Pond and Hells Bay. This canoe trail is excellent for those who either have limited time or for novice paddlers who want to sharpen their skills in a quiet protected area. It is also excellent when wind makes paddling elsewhere too challenging. Proceed slowly because there are quite a few sharp turns that may be challenging with longer canoes or kayaks. The trail winds through mangroves and narrow creeks that connect to a few small ponds. Watch for mangrove cuckoos, warblers, white-crowned pigeons, and night-herons along the trail.

Noble Hammock was once the site of a bootlegger's illegal whiskey still. William "Willie" Nobles built his whiskey still along this narrow creek, and it became a popular camp. He also was the proprietor of Nobles Bakery, Meat Market and Grocery in Homestead, which opened shortly after the turn of the twentieth century and remained until it was sold in 1913. Even as late as 1968, remnants of the whiskey still were present at Noble Hammock, which consisted of a wood boardwalk made of barrel staves, a brick furnace, a shallow well as a water source, and metal containers complete with deep gashes made by a law-enforcement officer's axe. Whiskey stills dotted the Everglades region during Prohibition (1920–33), and some were even built in deep solution holes of hammocks to hide them from the authorities. The lawlessness of the Everglades in those days was rampant, with locals poaching wildlife, shooting plume birds for the millinery trade, making moonshine, and committing murder. The rule of the day was that if you encountered anyone in the Everglades, always state why you're there but never ask them what they're doing out there, or you may never be seen again. When asked by government agents about their source of income, most claimed to be "farmers" because they grew sugarcane to make their moonshine.

Note: In 2012 a creek was cleared that connects the Noble Hammock Canoe Trail to West Lake, but because the National Park Service did not officially sanction this creek clearing, it is being allowed to become overgrown again.

11 Hells Bay Canoe Trail

Trailhead GPS coordinates: N25 13' 56.97" / W80 49' 23.69"

Type of trail: Canoeing or kayaking

Type of adventure: Enjoy a protected canoe or kayak excursion through a mangrove estuary. Opportunities for camping and fishing are available.

Total distance: From the trailhead: 3.0 miles to Lard Can campsite, 4.0 miles to Pearl Bay chickee (wheelchair accessible), 6.0 miles to Hells Bay chickee, 8.5 miles to Lane Bay chickee

Charts: Use NOAA Chart #11433 (Whitewater Bay) for navigating; *National Geographic Trails Illustrated Map #243: Everglades National Park* shows the trail. A GPS is advised.

Difficulty: Easy to moderate

Time required: A half to full day, depending on how far you decide to paddle (longer, of course, if you are camping)

Special considerations: Salt-marsh mosquitoes can be painfully maddening in summer and fall at the launch site, but their numbers generally dissipate to more tolerable levels (or not!) once you are on the water. Backcountry permits are required for camping.

Scenic value: Good. The trail meanders through red mangroves interspersed with saw grass and salt-marsh vegetation.

Overview and Route Description

The trailhead is located between Noble Hammock and West Lake on the north side of the main park road and is marked with signage. The trailhead has a small dock for loading and unloading and is located in a sheltered dome of mangroves. Besides mosquitoes, deerflies and horseflies can be particularly tormenting at the trailhead, especially in spring and early summer. Old-timers used to complain that Hells Bay was "hell to get into and hell to get out of," but that's not so true today with the marked trail and campsites now available to paddlers.

If you plan on camping, Lard Can is a land-based campsite, and Pearl Bay, Hells Bay, and Lane Bay are elevated wood chickees. There are some tight turns along this trail so long kayaks and canoes may have difficulty maneuvering. Otherwise, it is a nice protected trail that is a good choice when winds are strong. Fishing can be excellent as well, and fish to target in this area are mangrove snapper, snook, and redfish. Be advised that

Hells Bay Canoe Trail

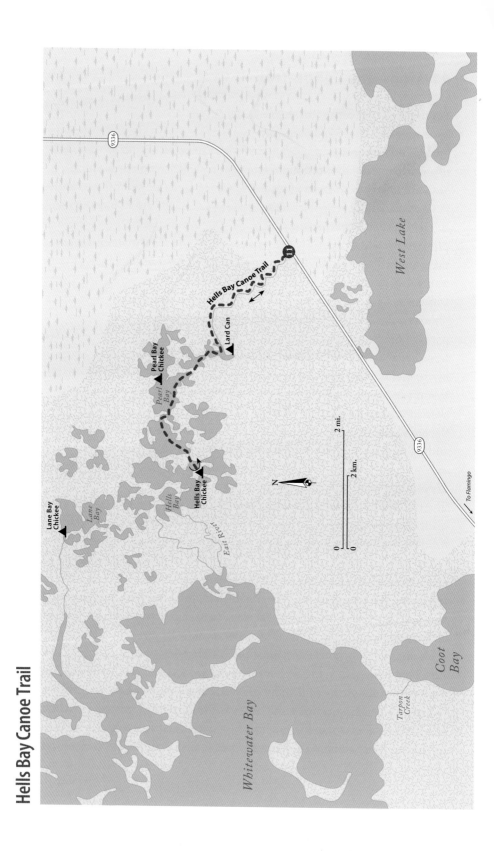

The Hells Bay region is a puzzling and somewhat intimidating maze of mangrove islands, creeks, and small bays.

powerboats can access portions of this area from Whitewater Bay, but motors are prohibited from the trailhead to the Lard Can campsite. Lard Can is limited to ten campers, Pearl Bay chickee (wheelchair accessible) is limited to six campers on each side of the chickee, and the same is true for Hells Bay chickee. Lane Bay is limited to six campers. Whitewater Bay can be accessed from the Hells Bay chickee by following the East River westward, and this could be a planned loop back to Flamingo. Once you reach Whitewater Bay, Flamingo is a 6.5-mile paddle. For this loop you will need to leave a vehicle at Flamingo to return to the Hells Bay trailhead.

If you decide to explore off the marked trail in the Hells Bay region, be absolutely certain that you do so with sensible caution. This is an area where you can become impossibly lost in very short order (look at your chart and you'll see why). The Hells Bay area is a complex and confusing maze of mangrove islands, creeks, lakes, and ponds that all look alike so check your chart and/or GPS often. It is highly advisable to stay on the trail if you are unfamiliar with the Everglades backcountry and especially if you are not in possession of a GPS unit (with spare batteries!) or at least a compass.

Although mangrove habitat is relatively repetitious, the wormvine orchid (*Vanilla barbellata*), dollar orchid (*Prosthechea boothiana*), butterfly orchid (*Encyclia tampensis*), and interesting bromeliads such as the powdery catopsis (*Catopsis berteroana*) can be seen along the Hells Bay Canoe Trail. The wormvine orchid blossoms are especially attractive and emit an enrapturing perfume, but the flowers appear in May and June, when only the hardiest (or craziest) paddlers venture out there. Admiring their beauty and heavenly aroma will require tolerating the horror of thousands of salt-marsh mosquitoes hell-bent on making you a part of their food chain. But once you see the flowers, all else will seem eclipsed, if only for a brief moment until the reality of summer in the mangroves returns. Look also for the mangrove rubber vine (*Rhabdadenia biflora*), which has single or paired white to pinkish, trumpet-shaped flowers and a yellow throat.

Note: There are four other chickees in remote areas east of Whitewater Bay and north of Hells Bay. Three of them can be reached via an inside route through the maze of mangrove islands from the Hells Bay chickee. These are the Lane Bay chickee, Roberts River chickee, and North River chickee. The fourth is the Watson chickee near the Watson River in the northeast corner of Whitewater Bay. All four can also be reached from Flamingo by taking Buttonwood Canal to Coot Bay and then entering Whitewater Bay through Tarpon Creek. Whitewater Bay can be very rough in windy conditions, so paddlers should be especially prepared.

12 West Lake to Alligator Creek Paddling Route

Trailhead GPS coordinates: N25 12' 53.02" / W80 51' 01.38"
Type of trail: Canoeing or kayaking (vessels with outboard motors of 6-horsepower or less are allowed in West Lake but not beyond)
Type of adventure: Canoe or kayak across open bays and through mangrove-lined creeks and ponds.
Total distance: 8.5 miles from the ramp at West Lake to the Alligator Creek campsite
Nautical Charts: NOAA Chart #11433 (Whitewater Bay); *National Geographic Trails Illustrated Map #243: Everglades National Park*
Difficulty: Moderate to strenuous, depending on wind conditions
Time required: 4 hours or more to reach the campsite
Special considerations: Mosquitoes and biting flies in summer and fall. Wind can create rough conditions for paddlers, especially in West Lake.
Scenic value: Excellent. The entire trail is lined with mangroves, and the creeks and ponds are very scenic.

Overview and Route Description

The entrance to the parking lot for West Lake is between Noble Hammock and Mrazek Pond along the main park road. A surface ramp, dock, picnic tables, and restroom facilities are available. There is also a short walking trail accessible from the parking lot (west side) that leads into mangrove habitat to an elevated wood dock overlooking West Lake. This is an excellent viewing station for a bonanza of ducks in wintertime. Fishing is prohibited from this dock.

When launching at the West Lake boat ramp, watch your footing because the ramp can be very slippery. This is an excellent paddle route as a day trip or to camp up to two nights (mid-November through late April) in a remote area along the aptly named Alligator Creek. Fishing can be excellent at times; the fish to target are spotted sea trout, snook, redfish, sheepshead, black drum, and mangrove snapper.

If winds are strong and you are in a canoe, stay close to the lee side of West Lake until you reach the protection of the creek that leads to Long Lake. If you are planning to travel the entire way to the Alligator Creek campsite, once you enter Long Lake, paddle southeast to the far side of the lake to Mangrove Creek, a narrow passage that leads to another lake called The Lungs (this lake has the shape of lungs when viewed from the air or on

West Lake to Alligator Creek Paddling Route

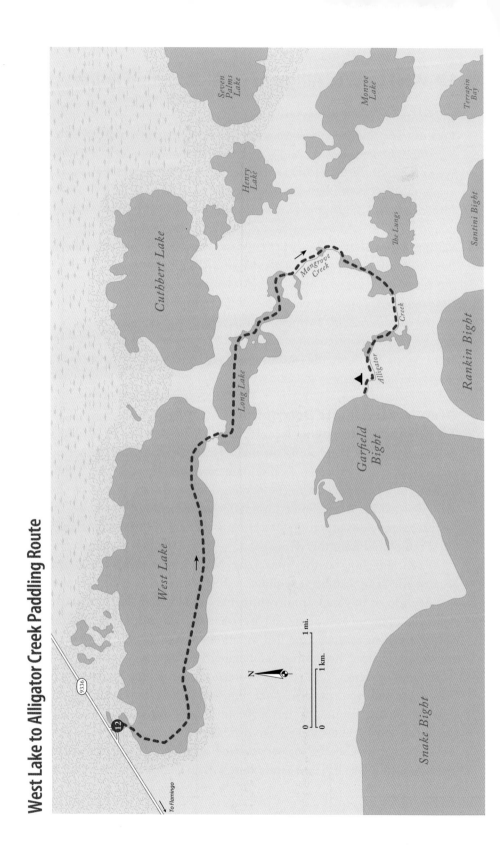

Picturesque West Lake at dawn

your chart). Stay close to the west shoreline of The Lungs until you reach Alligator Creek. Paddle west through the creek until you enter another small lake, and then paddle north until the shoreline forms a narrower passage. The next section of Alligator Creek leads to the campsite. This is a land-based campsite for up to three parties with a total of eight people. There are no toilet facilities. Sand flies (no-see-ums) can be especially bad at this campsite, so be prepared. Running and screaming are optional.

There are some very large American crocodiles in or near Alligator Creek, so give them a wide berth. One particularly large one likes to rest on a high marl bank and may come charging toward the water when it sees paddlers approaching, which can be quite unnerving to the uninitiated. Unlike Nile crocodiles of Africa and saltwater crocodiles of the western Pacific, our American crocodiles do not look at canoeists and kayakers as a food item, if this makes you feel any safer.

Alligator Creek opens into Garfield Bight, which can be a good place to see wading birds, especially during the beginning of a rising tide or the last stages of a falling tide. This bight is very shallow and may be impassable during low tide at full or new moon stages, so if the tide is falling just before dark, do not stray too far away from your campsite or you may find yourself stranded until the tide changes. Tide permitting, you can also explore Snake Bight, Rankin Bight, Santini Bight, and Florida Bay from this location. Fishing in this area can be exceptional. The principal fish to target include spotted sea trout, snook, and redfish. Sawfish (protected species), tarpon, and sharks also patrol these shallow waters. Bottlenose dolphins and West Indian manatees can sometimes be seen in the deeper passes of Florida Bay.

13 Snake Bight Trail

Trailhead GPS coordinates: N25 12' 04.12" / W80 52' 27.23"
Type of trail: Hiking or biking
Type of adventure: Hike or bike along an elevated trail through mangrove and coastal strand habitat to a wood overlook near the shoreline of Snake Bight.
Total distance: 1.6 miles one-way
Difficulty: Easy
Time required: 2 hours hiking; 1 hour biking, or longer if you are bird watching at low tide
Special considerations: Intolerable salt-marsh mosquitoes in summer and fall so be prepared
Scenic value: Good along the trail; excellent at the boardwalk overlooking Snake Bight

Overview and Route Description

The trailhead is located on the south side of the main park road between West Lake and Rowdy Bend and is marked with signage. The Snake Bight Trail overlook is a favorite among birders who want to view shorebirds, black skimmers, egrets, herons, roseate spoonbills, white pelicans (winter–spring), brown pelicans (all year), ospreys, bald eagles, and even greater flamingos that migrate to this area in winter. Binoculars are a must and spotting scopes are a plus. If you do not own a spotting scope, there are often birders there that do, and they never mind sharing.

Some visitors attempt to walk farther out to the shore of Snake Bight from the overlook for a better view, but this is not advised. The gray marl substrate has the consistency of cream cheese and can be more than knee-deep. It is best to stay on the overlook. There is a narrow channel that leads from the mangroves out into Snake Bight, and there are large alligators and crocodiles that use this channel at high tide to feed on mullet and other fish.

One interesting wading bird that can sometimes be seen feeding in the shallows here is the reddish egret. This long-legged bird feeds by spreading its wings and then running through shallow water after small fish. The animated flapping, stretching, and spinning are comical to watch. Mature reddish egrets have a grayish body and dull-red head and neck. Immature reddish egrets are white.

Snake Bight Trail

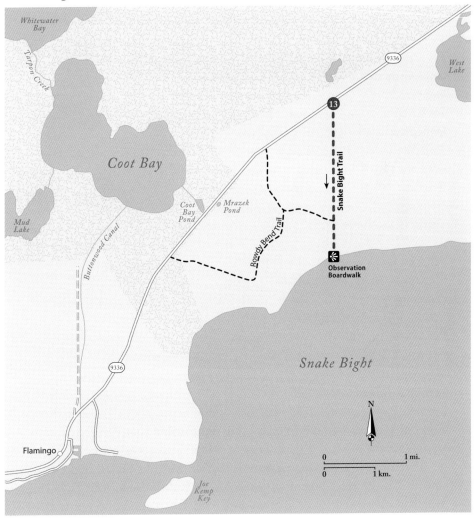

There are some interesting plants growing along this trail, including bromeliads and ferns as well as poison ivy, morning glories, and other plants that typify coastal strand and mangrove habitats. One small shrub of particular interest is the native bird pepper (*Capsicum annuum* var. *glabriusculum*). The tiny quarter-inch peppers are ten times hotter than jalapeños, but northern mockingbirds and gray catbirds gulp them whole with gusto. The peppers are red when ripe, so try one if you dare! Gulping

Exposed mud flats at low tide in or near Snake Bight become places for many species of birds to rest and feed.

water afterwards will not help. Be sure not to wipe your eyes if you happen to get the juice on your fingers, or you will be woefully sorry.

There is one prominent side trail leading west off Snake Bight Trail and this is the terminus of an extension of Rowdy Bend (see Trail 15), which also leads back to the main park road. It is a good hiking and biking trail as well.

Mrazek Pond

This small, shallow pond is marked with signage and is located right alongside the main park road. It is oftentimes a very worthwhile stopping place for birders. At times this small pond is dry and practically lifeless, but other times it literally teems with birdlife, especially coots, gallinules, an assortment of ducks, rails, egrets, herons, roseate spoonbills, white ibis, and other resident and migratory birds of the region. Look especially for blue-winged teal, green-winged teal, northern shovelers, American widgeon, ring-necked ducks, and pied-billed grebes. Brown pelicans and white pelicans even stop in for a meal at Mrazek Pond on occasion. It is most active in late fall, winter, and early spring and is a superb place for wildlife photographers to set up tripods and cameras with telephoto lenses. It will almost feel like cheating.

A flock of blue-winged teal tip their tails up as they feed in Mrazek Pond.

14 Coot Bay Pond to Mud Lake Paddling Route

Trailhead GPS coordinates: Coot Bay Pond: N25 10' 57.63" / W80 53' 52.51";
Mud Lake Creek entrance: N25 11' 25.07" / W80 55' 35.42"

Type of trail: Canoeing or kayaking

Type of adventure: Canoe or kayak across open water and through
mangrove-lined creeks.

Total distance: 7.0-mile loop from Coot Bay Pond

Charts: MapTech Waterproof Chart 28 (Flamingo to Everglades City); NOAA
Chart #11433 (Whitewater Bay); *National Geographic Trails Illustrated Map
#243: Everglades National Park*

Difficulty: Moderate to strenuous, depending on wind conditions. There is a
0.4-mile (700-yard) portage required.

Time required: 4 to 5 hours or more, depending on weather conditions

Special considerations: Mosquitoes and biting flies in summer and
fall. To complete the loop, there is a portage from Homestead Canal to
Buttonwood Canal. A few poisonous manchineel trees overhang the west
side of Buttonwood Canal before you reach Coot Bay (See "Hazards and
Health Warnings" in the introduction). Powerboats access the backcountry by
Buttonwood Canal but are required to slow down for canoeists and kayakers.
Show courtesy by paddling over to the shoreline for passing boaters as well
as the Everglades National Park tour boat. Strong winds can make Coot Bay
challenging for paddlers.

Scenic value: Excellent. There are scenic views of the Everglades
backcountry, narrow mangrove-lined creeks, and the opportunity for
excellent bird watching, especially in Mud Lake.

Overview and Route Description

This is a seldom-traveled loop trail that can be rewarding if the weather
is nice. Launch at Coot Bay Pond (on the right just past Mrazek Pond).
Once you cross Coot Bay Pond, you will enter a short, narrow creek that
leads to Coot Bay. Paddle toward the point ahead to your left about midway across Coot Bay, and use caution when crossing the marked channel that leads to Buttonwood Canal because of powerboat and tour boat
traffic (a no-wake zone is close to the entrance, so there should not be
any speeding boats in this area). Continue paddling west, and once you
round the point, continue on for 0.4 mile to a small creek on your left that
will lead you into Mud Lake. If the tide level is right in Mud Lake, you

Coot Bay Pond to Mud Lake Paddling Route

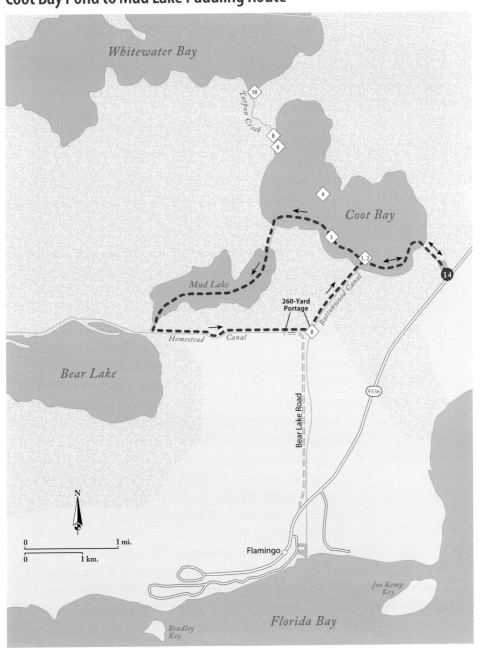

A group of white pelicans herd fish in Mud Lake. The white pelican is the second-largest bird in the United States.

might discover a variety of wading birds, including brilliant pink roseate spoonbills, feeding in the shallow water. If you enter Mud Lake at low tide close to a new moon or full moon, there may not be enough water to float a canoe or kayak. Your only two options are to wait for the tide to change and then continue on or turn around and explore Coot Bay. At higher tides Mud Lake is quiet, serene, and a place where you can see ducks, wading birds, white pelicans, and maybe an American crocodile or two. Paddle 1.5 miles across Mud Lake to a narrow creek marked by PVC pipes that leads to the historic Homestead Canal. Paddle through the creek and turn left (east) and take Homestead Canal to its terminus, where you will find a small dock to unload your gear if necessary. You will now have to portage your canoe or kayak due east 260 yards to a small dock at Buttonwood Canal. From there proceed north in Buttonwood Canal (watch for powerboat traffic), and when you reach Coot Bay, bear to the right and follow the shoreline to a marker at the creek that leads you back to Coot Bay Pond.

If you have the time, fishing in Coot Bay can be outstanding. Fish to target include spotted sea trout, snook, redfish, sheepshead, black drum, mangrove snapper, and tarpon. You can also choose to bypass the turnoff into Mud Lake and continue along the shoreline of Coot Bay to Tarpon Creek. This is a very scenic creek and popular fishing spot that connects to Whitewater Bay. Be advised that Whitewater Bay is aptly named so paddling in open water when the wind strengthens can very quickly turn your excursion into more exercise than you planned for, so paddle accordingly.

15 Rowdy Bend

Trailhead GPS coordinates: N25 10' 30.40" / W80 54' 18.06"
Type of trail: Hiking or biking
Type of adventure: Hike or bike along an elevated trail that leads through mangrove, salt marsh, and coastal strand habitats.
Total distance: 2.5-mile loop
Charts: *National Geographic Trails Illustrated Map #243: Everglades National Park*
Difficulty: Easy to moderate
Time required: 4 hours or more to hike the entire loop; 1.5 hours to bike it
Special considerations: Intolerable mosquitoes in summer and fall
Scenic value: Good. The trail is mostly tree lined, but there are some interesting native orchids, bromeliads, and other wildflowers that can be easily viewed.

Overview and Route Description

Rowdy Bend was once a road but is now a hiking and biking trail. The trailhead is on the south side of the main park road past Coot Bay Pond and is marked with signage. At the fork in the trail, turn to the right, the recommended route, to loop around to the main park road. (*Option*: The left fork leads to Snake Bight Trail and will lengthen your hike/bike by more than 2 miles. By turning right [south] on Snake Bight Trail, you can reach Snake Bight and the observation boardwalk there.) Most park visitors hike or bike for a distance and then turn around and return to the trailhead. Completing the entire loop requires hiking or biking along the main park road back to the trailhead, regardless of whether you stay on Rowdy Bend Trail or divert over to Snake Bight Trail. The scenery is relatively repetitious along the entire trail, but it is interesting nonetheless.

The northern cardinal is a common resident bird in the Everglades region. Listen for their distinctive chipping notes.

Rowdy Bend

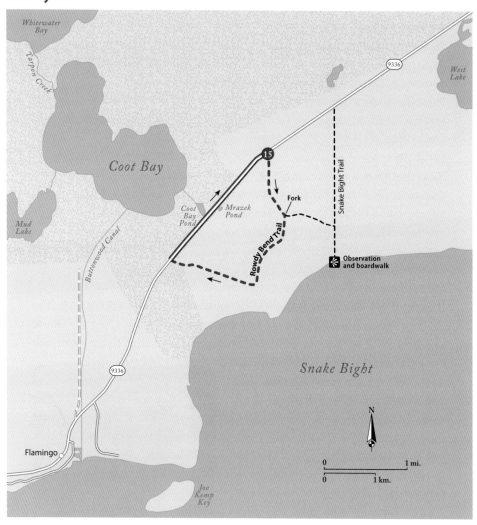

There are possibilities to see indigo snakes, eastern diamondback rattlesnakes, mangrove cuckoos, white-crowned pigeons, warblers, vireos, and other interesting wildlife.

16 Christian Point Trail

See map on page 20.
Trailhead GPS coordinates: N25 09' 05.68" / W80 55' 06.90"
Type of trail: Hiking. Biking is allowed but parts of the trail can be muddy, slippery, and tough to traverse on a bicycle.
Type of adventure: Hike through coastal mangroves and salt-marsh vegetation to Snake Bight.
Total distance: 4.0 miles round-trip
Charts: *National Geographic Trails Illustrated Map #243: Everglades National Park* shows the trail in an inset, but it is not detailed.
Difficulty: Moderate. The trail can be muddy at times.
Time required: 2 to 3 hours or more
Special considerations: Mosquitoes and biting flies in summer and fall
Scenic value: Excellent along portions of the trail; outstanding at Snake Bight

Overview and Route Description

Look for a narrow footpath marked by a sign on your left just before the bridge over Buttonwood Canal at Flamingo. This trail meanders through mangrove, salt marsh, and coastal strand habitats, terminating at Snake Bight east of Flamingo. Christian Point Trail is a nice, seldom-used trail and is also within walking distance of the Flamingo marina.

Check at the Flamingo Ranger Station for tidal conditions because if there is a falling tide or a low tide in Florida Bay, the Christian Point Trail can be an absolute showstopper for wading birds and shorebirds on the flats of Snake Bight (where the trail terminates). Bring binoculars or a spotting scope along with your field guide to birds. Here you might see a menagerie of shorebirds, terns, gulls, egrets, herons, roseate spoonbills, black skimmers, brown pelicans, white pelicans, and perhaps even greater flamingos. Overhead you should look for ospreys, bald eagles, and magnificent frigate birds.

It's such a nice place at times you may end up staying for hours. If nothing else, enjoy the peace and solitude as you watch the birdlife. There is a small bench at the end of the trail at Snake Bight.

The exposed mud flats in front of the Christian Point Trail in Snake Bight are outstanding places to see wading birds, pelicans, and a variety of shorebirds. If the tide is high in Snake Bight, many of these birds feed around the Eco Pond Loop, so it may be worthwhile to check there as well.

17 Eco Pond Loop

See map on page 20.
Trailhead GPS coordinates: N25 08' 19.38" / W80 56' 15.23"
Type of trail: Walking
Type of adventure: Walk along a loop trail that circles Eco Pond.
Total distance: 0.5-mile loop
Difficulty: Easy
Time required: 1 hour or more
Special considerations: Mosquitoes and biting flies in summer and fall. Very little shade.
Scenic value: Good. This is one of the most popular birding locations in Everglades National Park.

Overview and Route Description

The turnoff to Eco Pond is about 1 mile past the marina at Flamingo and is marked with signage on the right side of the main park road. The pond gets its name because it was once a natural filtration system for sewage water. It is one of the easiest places to see birds such as wood storks, roseate spoonbills, herons, egrets, bitterns, coots, ducks, gallinules, and a variety of shorebirds, including black-necked stilts and American avocets. Painted buntings can sometimes be seen here as well; these colorful migrants are present in southern Florida from about September into May. Watch also for bald eagles, short-tailed hawks, swallow-tailed kites, and other birds of prey soaring overhead.

There is a path that circles the pond, and if you are an avid birder, this is an excellent place to spend some time. An elevated wood boardwalk offers a place to rest and set up a camera tripod. Check at the Flamingo Visitor Center for reports of any unusual bird sightings around Eco Pond, or simply ask other birders along the trail. Some of the butterflies that can be seen along this trail include the silver-banded hairstreak, great southern white, eastern pygmy blue, ruddy daggerwing, zebra longwing, Julia heliconian, gulf fritillary, and a host of skippers.

Eco Pond is one of those places that require time and patience to explore. Sit for a spell and see what might happen right before your eyes. Keep your camera ready.

About Flamingo

Many people who visit Everglades National Park get the feeling that once they reach Flamingo, they have ended their Everglades adventure and they turn around and drive back. Actually, Flamingo can be the starting point for some of the best adventures available in the Everglades, so if you're looking for real wilderness adventure, Flamingo is a beginning, not an end. Buttonwood Canal leads north into the Everglades backcountry, where you can spend a day or even weeks exploring in a canoe, kayak, or powerboat. More adventurous explorers have even taken on the Everglades backcountry on paddleboards.

In front of Flamingo is Florida Bay, with a wealth of exploratory options available to visitors. Bird watching from a canoe or kayak can be especially rewarding in Snake Bight just east of Flamingo, especially at low tide when shorebirds and wading birds arrive to feed on crabs and other marine life stranded on the mudflats.

Flamingo was founded in 1893 when the society misfits, plume hunters, gator poachers, and moonshiners who lived there had to choose a name for the town in order to qualify for a post office. By 1910 there were forty-five hardy people living in this remote outpost, and most called themselves "farmers" because they relied on their sugarcane crops to make illegal whiskey, or moonshine. The only way to get to Flamingo in those days was by boat, so it wasn't a place often visited by law-enforcement officers, or anyone else for that matter.

There are many interesting stories about Flamingo—and some of them are even true. One true tale took place when Flamingo was overrun by rats, so a fellow named Gene Roberts took up a collection from Flamingo residents and sailed off to Key West. There he offered 10 cents for each cat that was brought to the dock, which ended up costing him $40. He then took the 400 cats to Flamingo in his sailboat, claiming it was the most dreadful trip he'd ever made in his life. Once he released his boatload of cats, they reportedly scattered in every direction, but the rat population did go away eventually.

Flamingo was also a place of murder and intrigue. There is a plaque located at the base of the stairs of the Flamingo ranger station that honors Guy Bradley, a onetime resident plume hunter who was appointed as the Monroe County deputy sheriff and game warden in June 1902. Bradley was murdered near the Oyster Keys, just

The Flamingo marina is a jumping-off point for backcountry and frontcountry paddling, fishing, and camping adventures.

offshore from Flamingo, by a plume hunter he was trying to arrest. The plaque reads:

> *Audubon warden was shot and killed off this shore by outlaw feather hunters, July 8, 1905. His martyrdom created nationwide indignation, strengthened bird protection laws and helped bring Everglades National Park into being.*

See Flamingo to Oyster Keys Historical Paddling Loop (Trail 21) in this guide for more information about Guy Bradley and for an opportunity to paddle to the location where he was murdered.

18 Coastal Prairie Trail

Trailhead GPS coordinates: N25 08' 12.08" / W80 56' 54.81"
Type of trail: Hiking or backpacking
Type of adventure: Hike or backpack on a trail through salt marsh and mangrove habitat along the edge of Florida Bay.
Total distance: Approximately 6.5 miles one-way to the Clubhouse Beach campsite; 13.0 miles round-trip. Camping is by permit only. Campsites are also accessible by canoe or kayak.
Difficulty: Moderate
Time required: All day to hike the entire trail and back
Special considerations: Mosquitoes and biting flies in summer and fall. Slippery trail when wet. Very little shade available.
Scenic value: Excellent. This trail offers a scenic view of coastal mangrove forests, extensive salt marshes, and Florida Bay.

Overview and Route Description

The trailhead is at the west side of Loop C in the Flamingo campground and terminates at Clubhouse Beach along the shore of Florida Bay. A backcountry permit is required to camp at East Clubhouse Beach (also accessible by canoe or kayak) or Clubhouse Beach campsites. It is possible to continue west along the shoreline from Clubhouse Beach, and intrepid explorers have even hiked all the way to Cape Sable, but this requires crossing House Ditch and the more formidable East Cape Canal. The only way across East Cape Canal is to hail a boater and hitch a ride to the other side (swimming across is highly inadvisable due to boat traffic, strong tides, crocodiles, and very large sharks). There is also a natural creek to contend with between East Cape Canal and East Cape Sable, but it is passable by wading across. Unless you are willing to endure a long and strenuous hike, it is best to access Cape Sable by canoe, kayak, sailboat, or powerboat.

The Clubhouse Beach campsites are scenic, but the waters of Florida Bay close to the shoreline are shallow and the bottom is muddy, so fishing is usually not very good at these campsites. Birding can be excellent and you will also see some interesting plants along the way. Everglades salt marshes are dominated by sea blite (*Suaeda linearis*), saltwort (*Batis maritima*), sea purslane (*Sesuvium portulacastrum*), annual glasswort (*Salicornia bigelovii*), and perennial glasswort (*Sarcocornia perennis*). The leaves of these plants are edible and have a salty taste. They are high in vitamin

Coastal Prairie Trail

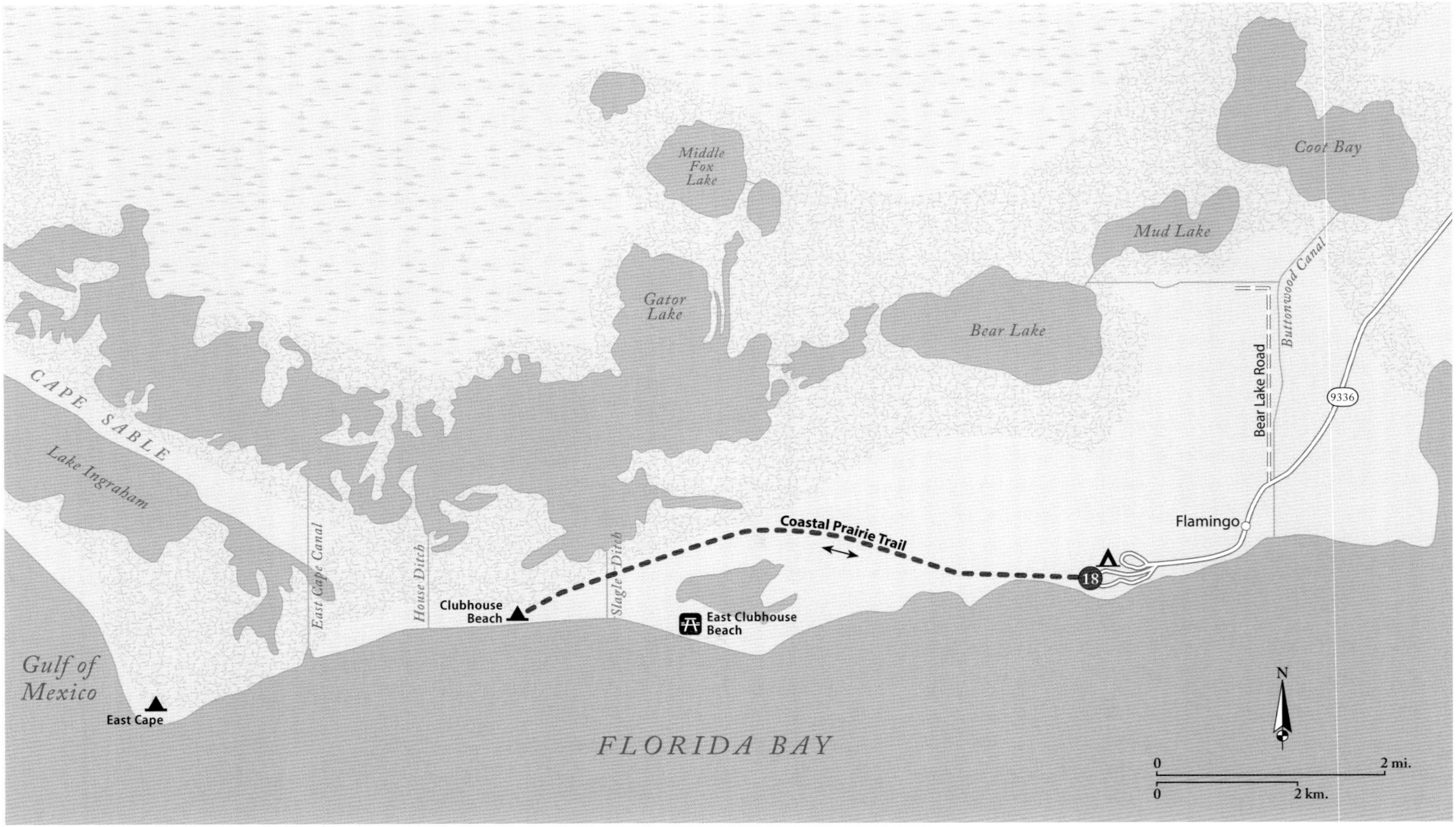

Cool Bay

Buttonwood Canal

9336

Mud Lake

Bear Lake Road

Bear Lake

Flamingo

18

Middle
Fox
Lake

Coastal Prairie Trail

Gator
Lake

Slagle Ditch

East Clubhouse
Beach

FLORIDA BAY

House Ditch

Clubhouse
Beach

East Cape Canal

CAPE SABLE

Lake Ingraham

East Cape

Gulf of
Mexico

N

0   2 km.
0   2 mi.

An osprey rests on the main park road near Flamingo before taking its prized catch back to its nest to feed two hungry chicks. Mullet . . . it's what's for dinner.

C and have been used to ward off scurvy, a disease caused by vitamin C deficiency. If a shrub called sweetscent (*Pluchea odorata*) is flowering, you will likely be treated to an abundance of butterflies. This aster relative has tiny heads of pink flowers and is an excellent nectar source for butterflies. Look for tropical buckeyes, mangrove buckeyes, great southern whites, mangrove skippers, white peacocks, and other coastal butterflies gathering nectar from the flowers. The larvae of the eastern pygmy blue feed on saltwort leaves, so look for this exceptionally small butterfly flying low over its host plant.

Occasionally, American crocodiles can be seen along the shoreline of Florida Bay. And always be a bit cautious of eastern diamondback rattlesnakes if you decide to explore off-trail in salt-marsh habitat. This large and potentially life-threatening venomous snake feeds on marsh rabbits and rodents that live in salt marshes, so it is not unusual to find one lying patiently along the small trails made by these animals. The eastern diamondback rattlesnake is a wonderfully beautiful snake, but be sure to admire it from a safe distance if you should be so lucky to come upon one.

If you hike this trail in springtime, listen for the musical, ascending, buzzing calls of the prairie warbler and the sweet, high, melodious notes of the Caribbean (golden) race of the yellow warbler. Both nest in the mangroves in this region, and their calls can be heard from far away. You may also hear the high-pitched, three-parted calls of the black-whiskered vireo in springtime. Also watch for white-crowned pigeons, mangrove cuckoos, ospreys, magnificent frigate birds, and bald eagles.

19 Flamingo to Cape Sable Paddling Route

Trailhead GPS coordinates: N25 08' 32.51" / W80 35' 24.68"

Type of trail: Canoeing or kayaking (also accessible by sailboats and powerboats)

Type of adventure: Paddle across the shallow open water (close to shore) of northern Florida Bay from Flamingo to Cape Sable.

Total distance: 10.5 miles to East Cape, 4.5 miles from East Cape to Middle Cape, 5.0 miles from Middle Cape to Northwest Cape

Charts: MapTech Waterproof Chart 28 (Flamingo to Everglades City); NOAA Chart 11433 (Whitewater Bay); Waterproof Chart 39 (Lostmans River and Whitewater Bay); *National Geographic Trails Illustrated Map 243: Everglades National Park*; Waterproof Chart 33E (Florida Bay), including Florida Bay north to East Cape Sable

Difficulty: Moderate to strenuous

Time required: About 4 hours to East Cape Sable

Special considerations: Mosquitoes and biting flies. Strong winds create rough conditions for paddlers. There can be strong tidal flow, especially around the capes and at the entrance to East Cape Canal. Watch for powerboat traffic entering and exiting East Cape Canal and Middle Cape Canal. Shade is a rare commodity the entire length of Cape Sable.

Scenic value: Superb

Overview and Route Description

Although this is not a designated "trail" because it crosses open water, Cape Sable is a popular destination for both tourists and residents who want to explore and camp on one of Florida's most beautiful and pristine beaches. If you have never been to Cape Sable, you are in for a treat. Wind and tides are the two biggest obstacles you might need to overcome, especially for novice paddlers. Strong winds coupled with powerful tidal flow can create very challenging conditions for any paddler, regardless of strength and skills. The strongest winds throughout the year generally occur from about midday to late afternoon, so check the weather conditions and plan your trip accordingly. Leaving very early in the morning (even before dawn) may allow you to reach Cape Sable in comparatively calm conditions. Use common sense if you plan on paddling before sunrise—stay close to shore and have a required battery-powered light onboard in case you need to alert boaters of your presence. Even if you

Flamingo to Cape Sable Paddling Route/Highland Beach
Paddling Route/Oyster Keys Historical Paddling Loop

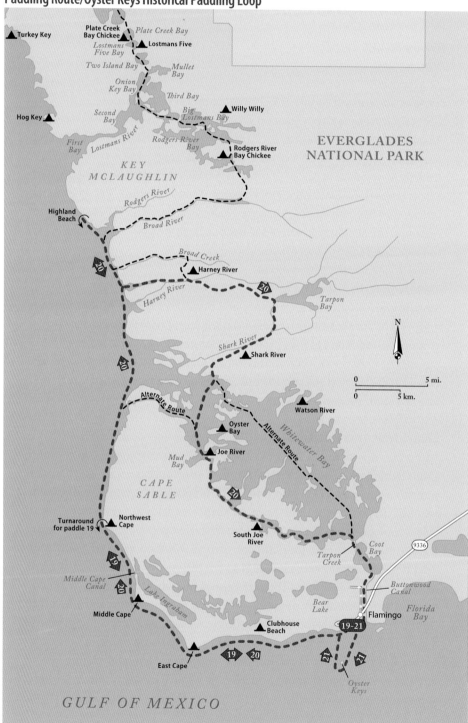

leave shortly after dawn, you will at least have a good head start before the wind picks up, or lucky you if it remains calm all day.

For those returning to Flamingo from Cape Sable when winds are strong out of the east or south, my best advice is to wait until nightfall and paddle back after dark when winds typically decrease. After you pass the first point sticking out into Florida Bay from the mainland, you should be able to see the red light on top of the radio tower at Flamingo. Point your bow at it and keep paddling.

There is, however, another option: If you are at Northwest Cape or Middle Cape, you can avoid at least some of the wind and chop by taking Middle Cape Canal (1.5 miles north of Middle Cape) into Lake Ingraham, following the marked channel southeast to East Cape Canal and then on to Florida Bay. This will place you about 1.4 miles east of East Cape Sable without having had to paddle in the open Gulf. Now you have a straight 9.2-mile paddle to Flamingo.

Middle Cape is especially scenic, and if you have the time to make the journey, Northwest Cape is the most peaceful and least-visited of the three capes. Cape Sable offers stunning sunsets, great fishing, and miles of pristine beach to explore. When deciding on a place to pitch your tent, first look for the long line of seaweed running parallel with the shore. This is called the wrack line, which is nothing more than sea debris left stranded at high tide. Be sure to pitch your tent landward of the wrack line or the ocean will come visit you in your tent during the next high tide. Also be advised that all campfires must be seaward of the wrack line (or at least close to it at high tide). To deter raccoons from running off with your supplies, secure your food and water before turning in for the night. If you have room, bring essential supplies (food, water) inside the tent. Styrofoam coolers are not a deterrent for hungry raccoons, nor are conventional coolers with plastic lid latches, so if you cannot bring your cooler inside your tent with you at night, tie it closed with rope and place it near your tent.

If you plan to fish for dinner, species to target include spotted sea trout, snook, redfish, mangrove snapper, black drum, pompano, and Spanish mackerel. Be sure to check seasonal closures and legal size limits for some species. Large sharks patrol these waters very close to shore while searching for a favorite food—stingrays—so swimming is ill-advised (and there are wicked rip currents around East Cape and Middle Cape).

Among the debris that washes up onshore, you may discover bits of charcoal-colored pottery shards left over from now-extinct native Americans who once roamed Cape Sable. It is here where the Tequesta territory met with the more warlike tribe, the Calusa, who were based in the Ten Thousand Islands region to the north. It was the Calusa who killed Juan Ponce de León in 1521. The last of the Tequesta fled Florida to Cuba in the mid-1700s to escape war, slavery, and the genocide of diseases introduced by Spanish explorers. Pottery shards are historical artifacts so leave them where you found them.

Interesting plants to look for along the beachfront of Cape Sable are sea lavender (*Argusia gnaphalodes*), bay cedar (*Suriana maritima*), sea oats (*Uniola paniculata*), and railroad vine (*Ipomoea pes-caprae*). *Everglades Wildflowers* (FalconGuides) will help you identify the native flora of this region. Enjoy your visit to Cape Sable—it is by far my favorite place in all of Florida.

Cape Sable is the southwestern tip of mainland Florida and offers stunning sunsets, camping along miles of pristine beaches, and great fishing. Lake Ingraham looms in the background.

20 Flamingo to Highland Beach Paddling Loop

In May 2010 I decided to take my new 16-foot 2-inch Swift Shearwater solo canoe on its maiden voyage, so I chose this route, which combined the open Gulf with more serene rivers and bays of the Everglades backcountry. My wife-to-be dropped me off at Flamingo and then proved she loved me by driving back ten days later to pick me up. It was such a grand wilderness adventure it deserves sharing with others.

See map on page 92.

Trailhead GPS coordinates: Flamingo, N25 08' 32.51" / W80 35' 24.68"

Type of trail: Open-water paddling along Florida Bay and the Gulf of Mexico and then paddling along tidal rivers and across open bays of the backcountry

Type of adventure: Canoeing or kayaking

Total distance: About 85 miles round-trip

Fees and permits: Check in at the Flamingo Visitor Center to pay backcountry camping fees and to receive your permit.

Charts: MapTech Waterproof Chart 28 (Flamingo to Everglades City); NOAA Chart #11433 (Whitewater Bay) and NOAA Chart #11432 (Shark River to Lostmans River) show the best detail; *National Geographic Trails Illustrated Map 243: Everglades National Park* is your next best choice.

Difficulty: Moderate to strenuous depending on weather and tidal conditions

Time required: 8 to 10 full days (or see "Alternate route" below)

Special considerations: Mosquitoes and biting flies in summer and fall. Storms can bring rough and potentially dangerous conditions, especially in the Gulf of Mexico. Watch for manatees in the rivers because they can flip a canoe or kayak with ease if you skid up on top of one (ask me how I know!).

Scenic value: Outstanding along the entire journey

Overview and Route Description

May is a nice time of year for this trip because weather patterns are more predictable, the rainy season has yet to arrive, it's warm enough to not need winter clothes, and you will likely not see one other soul camping out there. Sure, bugs will be less bothersome in the winter months, but you must pack for possible cold fronts that can bring wind, rain, cold fronts, and misery. Even 60°F when you're out on the water is cold, and I despise wearing winter clothes while paddling.

My campsite itinerary was East Cape Sable, Middle Cape Sable, Northwest Cape Sable, Shark Point, Highland Beach, Harney River chickee, Shark River chickee, Joe River chickee, and South Joe River chickee. This trip could be shortened by a day if you bypass Middle Cape Sable and paddle from East Cape to Northwest Cape, and it could be shortened by one more day by paddling the 17 miles from Northwest Cape Sable to Highland Beach, bypassing the Shark Point campsite at Graveyard Creek. There is a portable toilet at Shark Point, so you may want to pause for a pit stop on the way. On Highland Beach white-tailed deer not only stroll along the beach, they also wade out into the Gulf either to cool off or to avoid deerflies. At low tide they even graze on exposed sea grasses along the shoreline. And, if you choose the right time of year, you may be the only person camping for 40 miles in either direction. Where else in Florida can one find such blissful solitude?

Along the way, especially from the Shark River area to the Broad River, you will pass a large swath of dead mangroves. These are stark reminders of the fury of Hurricane Wilma, which struck southwest Florida in October 2005. They also serve as convenient lookout posts for ospreys and bald eagles.

The Rodgers River and the Broad River converge at the Gulf of Mexico on the south side of Highland Beach, so when you leave you will paddle across a wide expanse of flats where you may see bottlenose dolphins along with some very large sharks that ply these waters, cruising in and out with the tide. Your last four or five campsites have been on sandy beaches where there have been no navigation requirements other than keeping the shoreline to your right. That is about to change.

As you leave Highland Beach, paddle south and enter the north mouth of the Harney River. There is an exposed shell mound directly in the center of the river mouth. This is an excellent spot to get out and stretch, wash your clothes with biodegradable soap, submerge yourself in the water to cool off, and maybe do a little fishing. From here you will have a 4-mile paddle upriver to the Harney River chickee on the left.

This river is named to honor Lt. Col. William S. Harney, who led an expedition of ninety men in sixteen canoes in search of Chakaika, the war chief of the so-called Spanish Indians during the Second Seminole War. Chakaika and his men had attacked Indian Key in the Middle Florida Keys and killed Dr. Henry Perrine, so Harney was out for revenge. Harney surprised Chakaika while he was chopping wood at his camp, and

Storms move across the Gulf of Mexico off Highland Beach. It is imperative that paddlers pay attention to weather patterns in the Everglades, especially during the rainy season.

the nearest soldier shot him dead. Harney hung Chakaika's body from a tree and then moved southwestward toward the Shark River, where he planned to turn south to rendezvous with sailing ships off Cape Sable, but he instead discovered the river that now bears his name.

From the Harney River chickee, paddle east to the horseshoe bend that becomes the Shark River, then continue west about 4.4 miles to the Shark River chickee tucked inside a small cove on your left. Tides play an important part in determining whether this will be a leisurely excursion. If the tide is too strong, tie off to a mangrove branch and wait it out. It would be perfect if you left the Harney River chickee with an incoming tide and then caught the outgoing tide as you loop around into the Shark River. Timing is everything.

From the Shark River chickee, continue west toward the Gulf to the Shark River Cutoff, the first large passage to your left. Paddle through the cutoff until you see the large expanse of open water that is Oyster Bay (look for Channel Marker 51) and then keep south-southwest heading to the far end of Oyster Bay where it converges with the Joe River. Mud Bay will be on your right at this point, so turn southeast (left) and follow the river for about 0.6 mile to the Joe River chickee tucked away next to the mangroves on your left.

From the Joe River chickee, the key to staying in the river is to never take any tributaries to the left because all of them will lead you into Whitewater Bay. This leg of the journey is just over 6 miles, and eventually you will see a narrow creek angling off to the right (just beyond a large mangrove island in the center of the river) that leads to a hidden cove where you will find your accommodations for the evening, the South Joe River chickee. Get up early the following morning and paddle east to the headwaters of the Joe River where it connects to Whitewater Bay. If you dally too long, you may be facing easterly winds that can make your voyage more memorable than you'd like. Watch for the markers (or boat traffic) that indicate the entrance to Tarpon Creek. The distance from the South Joe River exit creek to Tarpon Creek is 5.25 miles. Outgoing tides in Tarpon Creek are relatively easy to paddle against so continue to Coot Bay and then follow the southern shoreline to Buttonwood Canal (indicated by markers). You now have about 2.5 miles straight down the canal to your journey's end at Flamingo. Mission accomplished!

Alternate route: If you do not have seven to ten days to spare, you can shorten it by paddling north along the Gulf from Northwest Cape and taking the Little Shark River into Oyster Bay. From there you can enter the Joe River and stay at the two chickees along its length. This would be a five- or six-day trip depending on whether you stayed two or three nights on Cape Sable.

21 Flamingo to Oyster Keys Historical Paddling Loop

On May 28, 1901, a Florida law was passed that made the killing of egrets, herons, cormorants, roseate spoonbills, and other nongame birds illegal, and it carried a fine of $5 for each offense, with an additional $5 fine for each bird, plus ten days in jail if it so pleased the judge. This was brought about because of the mass slaughter of plume birds for feathers to adorn fashionable women's bonnets. The killings usually took place in the breeding season and an ounce of feathers was more valuable than gold. In 1902 ex–plume hunter Guy Bradley assumed the dual role of Monroe County's game warden and the local deputy sheriff. Bradley lived in the fishing outpost called Flamingo and was paid $35 per month for his services.

One of the plume hunters was a man named Walter Smith and he was not about to let any law-enforcement officer tell him what he could and could not do for a living. On the morning of July 8, 1905, Bradley was home with his wife, Fronie, when he heard gunshots ring across Florida Bay. He walked out in front of his house and gazed 2 miles across the bay toward the Oyster Keys. Even from that distance he could make out Smith's blue schooner, the *Cleveland*. Smith's two sons were still shooting cormorants even while Bradley was rowing a skiff across the bay to arrest them. Later in the morning Fronie heard a single gunshot echo across the bay, not knowing it was a shot from Smith's .38-caliber Winchester that had just killed her husband. While Smith headed to Key West to turn himself in and claim self-defense, Bradley's skiff was drifting west in Florida Bay with his body slumped over inside. Five months after Smith murdered Bradley, he walked away a free man because the jury could not understand why shooting birds could possibly be illegal, and they bought Smith's lawyer's argument of self-defense.

Bradley's body was buried at Cape Sable, but a hurricane later washed the grave site into the sea. His headstone was eventually recovered and moved back to the Flamingo Ranger Station.

See map on page 92.

Trailhead GPS coordinates: N25 08' 32.51" / W80 35' 24.68"

Type of adventure: Paddle across open water of Florida Bay

Great blue heron feathers were worth their weight in gold during the early twentieth-century plume-hunting days around Flamingo.

Total distance: 4.0 miles round-trip

Charts: MapTech Waterproof Chart 28 (Flamingo to Everglades City); NOAA Chart #11433 (Whitewater Bay) shows the best detail; *National Geographic Trails Illustrated Map 243: Everglades National Park* is your next best choice.

Difficulty: Moderate, weather permitting

Time required: 3 hours round-trip

Special considerations: Mosquitoes and biting flies in summer and fall at the Flamingo boat ramp. Powerboat traffic in the main channel.

Scenic value: Excellent

Overview and Route Description

Paddle along the same route that Audubon warden Guy Bradley took on July 8, 1905, when he was murdered while trying to arrest plume hunters shooting cormorants next to the Oyster Keys. A good book to read about plume hunting and the murder of Guy Bradley is *Death in the Everglades* by Stuart B. McIver (University Press of Florida, 2003). While paddling around the Oyster Keys, look for egrets, herons, roseate spoonbills, cormorants, and white ibis. They may be distant offspring of the birds Bradley helped protect. Close your eyes and try to imagine hearing the gunshots.

To reach the Oyster Keys from the Flamingo marina, paddle south into Florida Bay, then veer to your right to avoid paddling in the marked channel that is used by powerboaters. Directly across Florida Bay to the south, you will see a large mangrove island called Murray Key. Look to the right of Murray Key and there you will see two small islands positioned next to each other. These are the Oyster Keys. It should take you about 45 minutes to paddle there. Then you can spend as much time as you like paddling around them, either sightseeing, fishing, or reading chapter 20 in *Death in the Everglades*, entitled "Shootout at Oyster Keys." (Unlike Bradley's, your voyage will be round-trip.) On your way back paddle due south to the small key just offshore of the Flamingo campground. It is called Bradley Key and will make your historical tour complete.

If you are camping in the Flamingo campground and you own your own canoe, kayak, or paddleboard, you can launch directly off the shoreline of the campground. The Oyster Keys will be due south and Bradley Key will be immediately to your right.

22 Everglades Wilderness Waterway

Trailhead GPS coordinates: Flamingo: N25 08' 32.51" / W80 35' 24.68"; Gulf Coast Visitor Center: N25 50' 43.62" / W81 23' 14.11"

Type of trail: Canoeing or kayaking

Type of adventure: Paddle along a marked trail to backcountry campsites.

Total distance: 99.0 miles one-way

Fees and permits: Check in at the Flamingo Visitor Center or the Gulf Coast Visitor Center to pay backcountry camping fees and to receive your permit.

Charts: MapTech Waterproof Chart 28 (Flamingo to Everglades City); NOAA Chart 11433 (Whitewater Bay) for the southern portion; NOAA Chart 11432 (Shark River to Lostmans River) for the central portion; NOAA Chart 11430 (Lostmans River to Wiggins Pass) for the northern section. There are also two waterproof charts that cover the same area that show GPS coordinates, but the scale is smaller than the NOAA charts. These are Everglades & Ten Thousand Islands (Chart 41) for the northern region, and Lostmans River & Whitewater Bay (Chart 39) for the southern region. You can also use *National Geographic Trails Illustrated Map #243: Everglades National Park*.

Difficulty: Moderate to strenuous depending on tides and weather conditions

Time required: Plan on at least 7 days by canoe, 5 days or more by kayak

Special considerations: Intolerable salt-marsh mosquitoes in summer and fall, especially at night. Biting flies can also be present along beach areas during the day throughout the year. There can be strong tides and swift currents in rivers that connect to the Gulf of Mexico. Wind can be a problem in open water. Summer thunderstorms and winter cold fronts can change conditions quickly.

Scenic value: Excellent. This is one of the best wilderness excursions in all of Florida.

Overview and Route Description

The Everglades Wilderness Waterway is real wild Florida and is by far my favorite paddling route in the Everglades. The trail begins at Flamingo for those heading north, or at Everglades City (or Chokoloskee Island) for those heading south. There are private services at Everglades City that will rent canoes and either pick you up when you arrive at Flamingo or transport you and your gear back to Everglades City.

Everglades Wilderness Waterway

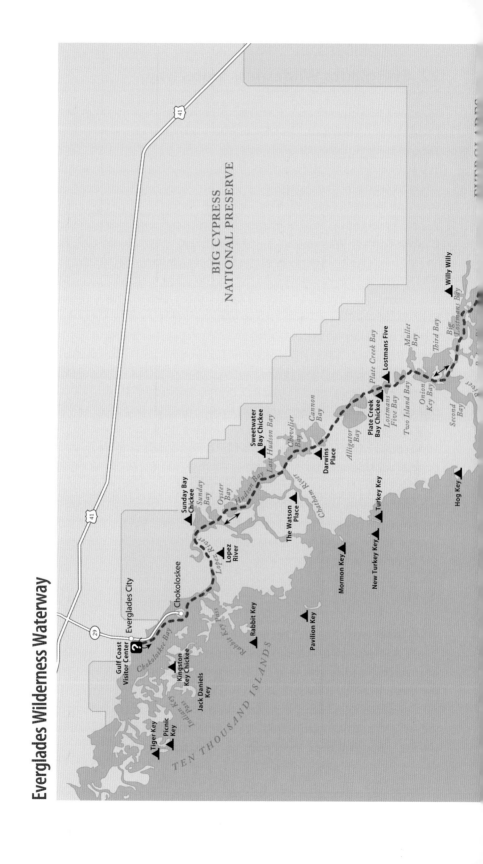

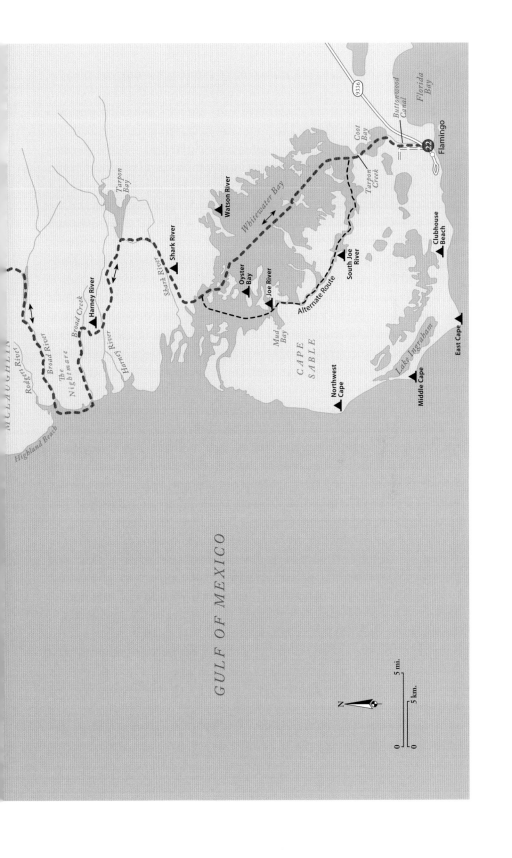

Everglades National Park backcountry camping permits are mandatory. Have your itinerary planned when you show up at the ranger station because once your itinerary is entered into the park computer, you will know right away whether or not your chosen campsites are available for you or your group. If you are attempting the trip in December or January, you may need to adjust your itinerary by either choosing other campsites or even scheduling more than one night at a campsite until the next one is available (some campsites are only available for one-night stays). Distances between campsites vary, but most are less than 10 miles apart and can easily be reached in 5 hours or less.

Plan for at least seven days, and do not treat this trip frivolously. Definitely do not overestimate your paddling abilities, so if you are a novice paddler, sharpen your skills elsewhere before attempting such a long and potentially grueling trip. Tides can be especially difficult to paddle against, plus violent storms and cold fronts can arrive quickly and bring rain, lightning, and strong winds without much advance warning. One unexpected mishap can change your trip from peaceful to miserable in short order. Safely exploring the Everglades backcountry requires careful planning and preparation, so check with park rangers for advice if needed.

If you purchase NOAA charts (the best in my opinion because of the larger scale than the waterproof charts), cut the charts into sections and have them laminated. This protects them from water damage and makes the charts easier to use. Be sure to label the top, bottom, and sides of each section so you will know which one connects to the other. Put them in a binder of some sort and you're all set.

There are more than thirty campsites available along the Wilderness Waterway, with over twenty of them land-based. The others are elevated chickees that consist of a wood dock with a roof and portable toilet (most are double chickees for two groups of campers). Instead of following the marked Wilderness Waterway through the interior of the Everglades, it is possible to skirt the Gulf coast, where paddlers can stay at land-based campsites. This places paddlers in a much more exposed situation should the weather act up, which can prove to be perilous. The outside route is far safer in a kayak than a canoe. Whichever route you take, always have an alternative plan.

Be well aware that the area called The Nightmare is impassable at low tide, and even in a canoe you will be left stranded in mud where portaging

Elevated wood chickees average about 10 miles apart along the Everglades Wilderness Waterway and offer a dry place to camp, protection from the sun, and toilet facilities. Most are double chickees to accommodate two groups of campers.

is impossible. If you are about to enter The Nightmare and the tide is falling, you should either take the outside route from the Broad River to the Harney River along the edge of the Gulf of Mexico, weather permitting of course, or wait until the tide changes. The Nightmare is nothing more than a narrow winding creek through a dense mangrove forest, so don't think it's somehow any spookier than other creeks along the waterway. If you do get stranded in The Nightmare at low tide, you have a couple of hours to watch fiddler crabs in the exposed mud along with mangrove crabs crawling around on the trees while you wait for the tide to change. On occasion you may have to portage over fallen trees.

In the northern half of the Wilderness Waterway, especially when crossing some of the larger interior bays, pay very close attention to the markers because they are smaller and less visible than those in the southern half of the waterway. If islands are not matching up to those on your chart, stop and hold your position until you get it figured out, even if you have to backtrack to the previous marker. It is wise to have binoculars onboard for this very purpose, and a GPS. Another tip is to sit and watch for powerboats traversing the marked waterway and then paddle accordingly.

Some Nice Overnight Paddling Trips in Everglades National Park
The following paddling excursions will give you some brainstorming ideas about where to paddle for overnight or two-night outings in Everglades National Park's backcountry and front country. Permits are required. See also the Hells Bay Canoe Trail in this guide.

Everglades City to Picnic Key: 7.3 miles one-way

Chokoloskee Island to Rabbit Key: 5.75 miles one-way

Chokoloskee Island to Pavilion Key: 9.0 miles one-way

Chokoloskee Island to Lopez River campsite: 4.0 miles one-way

Chokoloskee Island to Watson Place campsite: 17.0 miles one-way

Flamingo to South Joe River chickee: 11.5 miles one-way

Flamingo to Shark Point chickee (Florida Bay): 7.5 miles one-way

Flamingo to Johnson Key chickee (Florida Bay): 6.25 miles one-way

Flamingo to East Clubhouse Beach: 4.5 miles one-way

Flamingo to East Cape Sable: 11.0 miles one-way

The author's Kevlar canoe on Cape Sable packed for a 10-day solo trip. Colored bags help organize gear.

Useful Tips about Paddling the 99-Mile Everglades Wilderness Waterway

Canoe or kayak? You have a choice of paddling options. I much prefer canoes for long-distance paddling because you can pack more gear, plus your gear is more accessible. The benefits of kayaks are that they are more seaworthy in rough conditions, they are less prone to wind because of their lower profile, many are equipped with a rudder to avoid wind-cocking, and your gear can be stowed securely inside the hull. Kayaks are generally faster than canoes, but that really depends on the canoeist and the type of canoe he or she owns. Narrow solo canoes are typically much lighter in weight than kayaks and can be equally fast. Although the word "fast" relates to speed, it also equates to ease of paddling, which means you can cruise at a leisurely pace using less effort. Plastic canoes and kayaks are heavier and slower than their counterparts made of fiberglass, Kevlar, or carbon fiber.

(continued on next page)

As for paddles, buy the lightest paddle you can afford. The lighter the better because you will be paddling with it for many hours each day and heavy paddles will create sore muscles and fatigue. Expect to pay $150 to $400 or more for a good, lightweight kayak or canoe paddle. I use an Epic carbon fiber kayak paddle in my Kevlar solo canoe, and I always carry a lightweight canoe paddle as an emergency backup or to use in winding, narrow creeks.

Water is the most crucial item to bring along. The rule of thumb is one gallon of water per person per day with one additional gallon per person per week. This would mean that a solo paddler should bring eight gallons of water for a seven-day trip. I recommend bringing an extra half gallon per person per day in the summer months. I usually add powdered Gatorade to the water, which hydrates better than plain water and replenishes electrolytes lost in sweat. Purchase one-gallon plastic jugs and tie or bungee the handles to the thwarts of your canoe in case you flip. If you are in a kayak, stash the jugs both forward and aft to balance the weight. Remember that water weighs about 8.5 pounds per gallon, but at least you will be lightening the load with each passing day. Also bring some of your water into your tent with you at night to avoid thirsty raccoons marauding your stash if you are at a land-based site. And bring an empty jug inside your tent to pee in at night to avoid the potential problem of baring parts of your body to hordes of mosquitoes and then bringing them back into the tent with you. Women should bring a funnel and tube to make that task easier.

As for food, I prefer to pack fresh produce like asparagus, carrots, celery hearts, potatoes, corn in the husk, citrus, apples, and dried fruits and nuts. Remove the fresh fruits and vegetables from their packaging and wash them before packing them in two-gallon sealable plastic bags that can be stowed out of the sun. If you're not a vegetarian, consider beef or turkey jerky and sealed packages of tuna and salmon that do not require refrigeration. Hard-boiled eggs can last a few days without refrigeration, as can smoked fish. Other good choices are bagged soup mixes and other dried meals that don't require very much water. Dried, packaged soups and pasta dishes are excellent, and you can burn the packages they come in so there's no trash to haul out. Try to avoid canned or bottled food items, or at least keep them to an absolute minimum. You can even buy wine in cartons to avoid glass bottles.

A spotted sea trout was caught on the very first cast of the morning off the beach of Middle Cape Sable.

Of course, catching your own fresh fish is always a great option, so bring your favorite fishing rig along with lures and jigs. Surface lures that dive shallowly when retrieved are good choices, as are weighted rubber shrimp.

Always, or rather *ALWAYS*, bring a spare paddle and tether yourself to your canoe or kayak, plus tie all of your gear down in case you should flip. In fact, pack your canoe as if you expect to flip so you'll be better prepared for the event should it happen. If you skid up onto the back of a manatee in a river by accident, consider yourself flipped. To prepare yourself prior to your trip, flip your canoe or kayak in deep water and practice getting back inside (this can be done in a swimming pool).

There are mesh coverings to place over your gear in canoes to help keep everything secure, and bungee cords help too. Sunscreen is an absolute must, and you need to wear comfortable cotton or quick-drying clothes. Lightweight cotton pajama bottoms are great paddling pants for warmer weather, and lightweight, baggy, long-sleeved shirts are good choices to help ward off the sun.

The best chart is MapTech Waterproof Chart 28 (Flamingo to Everglades City).

Everglades National Park, Shark Valley

Shark Valley
36000 SW Eighth St. (Tamiami Trail)
Miami, FL 33194
Phone: (305) 221-8776
Website: nps.gov/ever/planyourvisit/svdirections.htm

THE SHARK VALLEY ENTRANCE IN EVERGLADES NATIONAL PARK IS located 19 miles west of Krome Avenue (SR 997) on Tamiami Trail (US 41) or 75 miles east of Naples. There is an entrance station, visitor center, bookstore, and a concession that rents bicycles and operates a tram. Rangers and volunteers also offer guided walks.

Hours of Operation

The Shark Valley gate is open from 8:30 a.m. to 6 p.m. daily from mid-December to mid-April and from 9 a.m. to 6 p.m. during the off-season. The Shark Valley Visitor Center is open from 8:30 a.m. to 5 p.m. daily. The parking lot closes at 6 p.m., so be sure to plan your trip so you arrive back before then. Entry before 8:30 a.m. or after 6 p.m. is allowed for walk-in visitors and cyclists. There is no fee for entry before or after hours, but be sure to park outside of the posted No Parking signs at the park entrance or the Miccosukee police may issue you a parking ticket. Parking is not allowed close to the entrance because cars block the view of oncoming traffic on Tamiami Trail.

Fees

For current entrance, bicycle-rental, and tram ride fees, please phone the Shark Valley Visitor Center at (305) 221-8776, or check the Everglades National Park website (nps.gov/ever).

Everglades National Park Shark Valley Overview

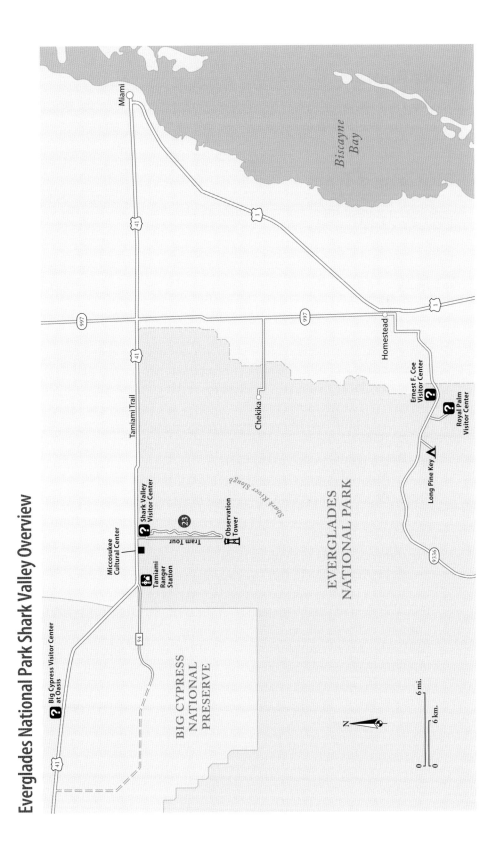

Bike Rentals

Bicycles can be rented from a private concessionaire at Shark Valley. Rentals are available from 8:30 a.m. to 4 p.m., and all bikes must be returned by 5 p.m.

Motorized Tram

The 2-hour guided tram tour is available all year, but times of operation vary with the season. The tram runs every hour from 9 a.m. until 4 p.m. daily, but during peak season it may run every half hour.

Safety

- Bicycle helmets are required by Florida law for children age 16 and younger.
- Always maintain a safe speed on bicycles, not only for your safety (and the safety of other bikers and hikers) but also for the well-being of wildlife that might be crossing or lying on the trail. Besides, it is much more enjoyable to travel at a leisurely pace and enjoy the wildlife, wildflowers, and scenery along the trail.
- Always hike and bike against the flow of tram traffic. The tram travels the trail in a clockwise direction, so hikers and bikers should travel up the straight paved trail that leads due north from the visitor center. This will allow you to see the trams coming and step off the trail. You are required to come to a complete stop and step off to the right of the trail when a tram approaches.
- Very large alligators sometimes lie on or near the trail. Give them a wide berth (at least 15 feet) when going around them. If this much room is not available, wait until it moves or wait until the tram comes along and frightens it off the trail. Be advised that it is unlawful to harass alligators in any manner.
- Always be sure to take plenty of water along on your trip, especially if you plan on completing the entire 15-mile loop. Sunscreen, mosquito repellent, and a hat are also advised.
- Roller skates, in-line skates, and skateboards are not allowed on the Shark Valley Trail.
- It seems ridiculous to say, but the speed limit for cyclists on the trail is 25 mph.

23 Shark Valley Trail

Trailhead GPS coordinates: N25 45' 42.14" / W80 45' 59.18"
Type of trail: Hiking, biking, or tram
Type of adventure: Hike, bike, or ride a tram on a paved trail through a vast Everglades marsh. The trail is a nature photographer's playground.
Total distance: 15.0 miles round-trip
Difficulty: Easy to moderate on a bicycle, depending on wind speed and direction
Time required: Allow for 3 hours to complete the loop on a bicycle. Most visitors spend their time walking slowly along the canal to observe wildlife and then turn around and return to the trailhead.
Special considerations: Mosquitoes and biting flies in summer and fall. Large alligators sometimes lie on the trail. Bring sunscreen and plenty of water because there is not much shade.
Scenic value: Outstanding, especially from the observation tower at the end of the trail

Overview and Route Description

The trailhead is at the west end of the parking lot by the canal. If you are a birder, you will want to hike or bike slowly with frequent stops. Typical birds to look for include common moorhens, egrets, herons, anhingas, and red-shouldered hawks. Specialty birds include snail kites, wood storks, roseate spoonbills, purple gallinules, least bitterns, American bitterns, limpkins, and rails. Black-crowned night herons and yellow-crowned night herons can also be seen here, even during the daytime. Look also for warblers, vireos, and other migratory birds from fall through spring.

Alligators are common along the trail and baby alligators can be seen seasonally, often crowded together in groups with their protective mothers nearby. Watch for water snakes, including venomous cottonmouth moccasins, along with various species of freshwater turtles. Fish abound in the canal along the trail, but not all of them are welcome. The aquarium trade and fish farms are responsible for the release of numerous exotic fish from around the world into Florida waters, and many of those species now reside permanently in the Everglades. Look for Mayan cichlids, oscars, walking catfish, and blue tilapia among the native largemouth bass, spotted gars, sunfish, and mudfish. Otters and even bobcats are sometimes

Shark Valley Trail

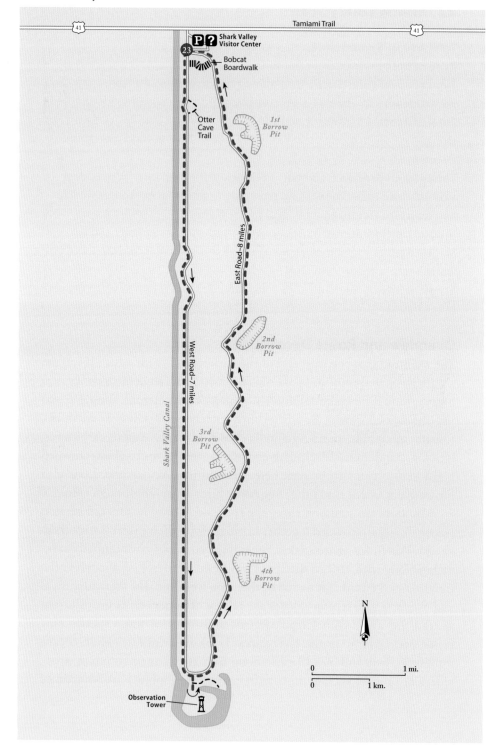

Tamiami Trail
41

P ? Shark Valley
Visitor Center

23

Bobcat
Boardwalk

Otter
Cave
Trail

1st
Borrow
Pit

East Road–8 miles

2nd
Borrow
Pit

West Road–7 miles

3rd
Borrow
Pit

Shark Valley Canal

4th
Borrow
Pit

N

0   1 mi.

0   1 km.

Observation
Tower

The purple gallinule is one of the most sought-after birds in the Everglades. Birders flock to Shark Valley each winter to see them.

seen at Shark Valley, so it's always a good idea to move quietly to have the best chance of seeing these or other interesting animals.

Along the Shark Valley Trail are two secondary trails that are worth exploring. These are the Bobcat Boardwalk and Otter Cave Trail, each only about 0.3 mile long. They will both be on your left as you hike or bike southward on the trail.

The first half of the trail is relatively straight and leads to a tall observation tower (restrooms available) where you can get a bird's-eye view of Shark Valley—a wide swath of saw grass that channels water southwest to the Shark River and eventually into the Gulf of Mexico. This freshwater is vitally important for the biologically rich mangrove forests and estuaries of Florida's southwest coast. The tower is 7 miles from the trailhead. If you are completing the loop, the eastern half of the trail meanders past four "borrow pits," which are artificial ponds created when limestone was excavated to construct the elevated road for oil exploration. These artificial ponds are habitat for a wide range of wildlife.

The tram offers a slow, comfortable ride with frequent stops while interpreters identify wildlife and explain points of interest along the way. Interpreters are private concession employees, park rangers, or volunteers, so be sure to thank them for their services. If you want a relaxing way to see Shark Valley, the tram is the way to go.

It is still possible for intrepid explorers to make their way south and west by canoe through the saw grass of Shark Valley to Rookery Branch and on to Whitewater Bay and Flamingo, but this requires a great deal of familiarity with the region. It is also only passable during the summer rainy season and can easily become a trip filled with misery, fatigue, and countless questions about one's sanity. Sleeping in a canoe in the middle of a sea of saw grass surrounded by alligators and summer swarms of mosquitoes is not the height of camping comfort (and I am speaking from personal experience). It is certainly not a sanctioned trip by the park, and any mishap could become a dire emergency. It is best to observe this river of grass from either the tower at Shark Valley or the Pa-Hay-Okee overlook to the south, where you can imagine the hardships one would have to endure while attempting to cross this vast region.

Tamiami Trail Triathlon

If you have a competitive spirit or if you simply like challenges and outdoor recreation, then consider the Tamiami Trail Triathlon. To complete the triathlon, you must bicycle the entire 15-mile loop at Shark Valley, then hike a 3-mile loop from the Oasis Visitor Center along the Florida National Scenic Trail in the Big Cypress National Preserve, and finally paddle a 3.5-mile route from the Gulf Coast Visitor Center in Everglades National Park to Sandfly Key and back. Participants will receive a guide that mentions things to look for while taking part in each activity and then, after completing each one, participants must answer a question relating to each activity. Upon completion participants receive a prize for finishing the Tamiami Trail Triathlon. Participate alone, bring a friend, or make it a fun family outing. Inquire at Shark Valley, the Oasis Visitor Center, or the Gulf Coast Visitor Center for further details.

Biscayne National Park

Biscayne National Park
Convoy Point Headquarters
9700 SW 328 St.
Homestead, FL 33033
Phone: (305) 230-7275 (press 0 to speak to a ranger at the front desk)
Website: nps.gov/bisc
Hours of operation: Park entrance at Convoy Point, 7 a.m. to 5:30 p.m. daily;
Dante Fascell Visitor Center, 9 a.m. to 5 p.m. daily

> *Drifting over the Florida Reef on a quiet day one may note all the details of its tropical luxuriance twenty feet below, and feels himself afloat on a sort of liquid light, rather than water, so limpid and brilliant is it.*
>
> —Commodore Ralph Munroe,
> *The Commodore's Story*, 1930

JUAN PONCE DE LEÓN WROTE IN 1513 OF FINDING A "BRIGHT NAMELESS great bay and fresh springs" during his travels around the land he called *La Florida*, so named because it was discovered at Easter time, or Pascua Florida (Feast of Flowers). The people he encountered here were the Tequesta, numbering about 250,000, who lived off the natural riches of Biscayne Bay, harvesting oysters, clams, fish, spiny lobsters, West Indian manatees, and even now-extinct Caribbean monk seals. The bay was a bountiful source of food, complete with freshwater springs bubbling up from the Biscayne aquifer. Ponce de León called it *Chequescha* but it would later be called Biscayne Bay.

Biscayne Bay has a rich and diverse history, from its shoreline settlement by South Florida's most ancient people, the so-called Paleo-Indians, to habitation by such animals as Columbian mammoths, American mastodons, camels, peccaries, bison, dire wolves, American lions, South American spectacled bears, jaguars, saber-toothed cats, and even California condors. These were only some of the animals found at

Biscayne National Park Overview Map

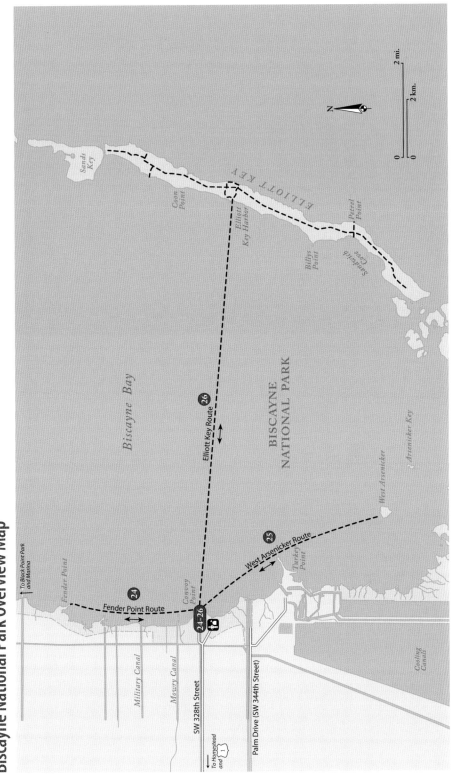

Biscayne Bay is a watery playground for canoeists, kayakers, boaters, anglers, and divers. Miami looms off on the horizon from Boca Chita Key in Biscayne National Park.

the Cutler Fossil Site along southern Biscayne Bay in the 1970s. Tequesta Indians later became the dominant people in this region and were the first indigenous people in Florida to see Spanish galleons appear offshore. Biscayne Bay also holds tales of Black Caesar the pirate, sunken ships, treasure hunters, drug smugglers, greedy developers, pineapple farmers, hurricanes, and more.

Today Biscayne Bay is a focal point and source of recreation for both local residents and more than 10 million tourists who travel to the Greater Miami area each year. But local developers and politicians once threatened this crown jewel. The proposed city of Islandia was to encompass Elliott Key (now in Biscayne National Park) and other islands that border Biscayne Bay and the Straits of Florida in the Upper Florida Keys. A causeway from Key Biscayne was to allow access to beachfront resorts and multimillion-dollar homes. Days before the island was to be turned over to the National Park Service, spiteful developers bulldozed a wide swathe directly down the center of Elliott Key, and this trail today is humorously called Spite Highway.

An even more preposterous scheme was to dredge the entire southern bay into a deepwater port so tankers and cruise ships could gain access through deep channels cut through offshore coral reefs. Luckily for the people of Florida, and for the flora and fauna of Biscayne Bay and the Upper Florida Keys, none of these misguided ventures made it past the planning stages. Much of the bay is now protected within Biscayne National Park, the very first national park that is mostly underwater. Whether you are a sailor, water-sports enthusiast, angler, or simply someone who likes to sit and meditate along the shores of Biscayne Bay, the result is still the same—pure pleasure.

Author's note: As of this writing, guided snorkeling and scuba-diving trips, island tours, glass-bottom-boat tours, and rentals of canoes and kayaks at Convoy Point are temporarily unavailable. The park is working to resolve the issue and regrets the inconvenience. Please contact the park for the current status regarding these services or visit nps.gov/bisc. Paddlers and boaters can still access Biscayne National Park on their own. In the meantime, if you are interested in snorkeling and scuba-diving trips, you may wish to visit John Pennekamp Coral Reef State Park at Mile Marker 102.5 on Key Largo.

The Dante Fascell Visitor Center in Biscayne National Park is located at Convoy Point. Access it off US 1 by taking North Canal Drive (SW 328th Street) 7.2 miles east to a turnoff on your left marked with signage for Biscayne National Park. This entrance road leads to a parking lot with access to the Dante B. Fascell Visitor Center. A wheelchair-accessible bookstore and information desk are located upstairs.

There is a surface ramp on the north side of the parking area that is available for canoeists, kayakers, windsurfers, and paddleboarders (motorized vessels must be launched at Homestead Bayfront Park). Launching paddle craft at Convoy Point is free of charge.

There are rocking chairs on the upper porch of the Dante Fascell Visitor Center to sit in and take in the breathtaking view of Biscayne Bay. If you want a closer look, follow the seawall around to a path that leads to a jetty. Here you can fish or just relax and enjoy the view. You can see Key Biscayne and Greater Miami looming off on the far horizon to the northeast and you can usually make out the tree canopy covering Elliott Key due east across the bay.

Biscayne National Park encompasses 172,971 acres of ocean, coral reefs, barrier islands, and coastal wetlands and is bordered to the south by

Parrotfish are among the most colorful fish you can see while diving in Biscayne National Park.

John Pennekamp Coral Reef State Park on Key Largo. Snorkeling over shallow reefs and wrecks or scuba diving on deeper reefs and wrecks are very popular activities within the park. On clear days, usually in summer, underwater visibility is 50 to 100 feet. Fishing for snapper, grouper, sailfish, marlin, dolphinfish (mahimahi), and a host of other game fish is also popular, as is diving for spiny lobster during open season, but lobster diving is banned inside Biscayne Bay (permitted in the ocean). Be sure to check the regulations that govern harvesting of spiny lobsters in Florida, and be advised that there are drowning deaths practically every year during recreational lobster season.

Tent camping is allowed on Elliott Key and Boca Chita Key. Camping permits are available in the Dante Fascell Visitor Center at Convoy Point. Adams Key, which borders Elliott Key to the south at Caesar's Creek, is available for day use and has restrooms, picnic tables, and grills. All islands in Biscayne National Park are only accessible from the water.

24 Convoy Point to Fender Point Paddling Route

See map on page 121.
Trailhead GPS coordinates: N25 27' 53.08" / W80 20' 07.77"
Type of trail: Canoeing, kayaking, or paddleboarding
Type of adventure: Paddle over sea-grass beds along the mangrove shoreline of Biscayne Bay with opportunities for bird watching, fishing, swimming, and snorkeling.
Total distance: 2.75 miles to Fender Point, 5.5 miles round-trip
Charts: *Waterproof Top Spot Miami Area Fishing and Diving Recreation Map* (#N211)
Difficulty: Easy with calm to moderate winds; moderately strenuous in stronger winds
Time required: Allow for 2 hours or more
Special considerations: Always be watchful for thunderstorms and waterspouts.
Scenic value: Excellent

Overview and Route Description

This leisurely route takes you from Convoy Point north along the shoreline of Biscayne Bay to Fender Point. From the Convoy Point ramp, paddle due north past the two spoil islands at Military Canal and then follow the shoreline north. If you have nice, calm weather, put on some polarizing sunglasses and paddle slowly along the shoreline to look for fish and other sea creatures along the way. You might see barracudas, spotted eagle rays, large stingrays, sharks, bonefish, permit, and perhaps even some bottlenose dolphins out in deeper water. Also look for blue crabs, spider crabs, puffers, and porcupine fish (do not disturb the crab traps along this stretch of shoreline). Fender Point will be the long, narrow point protruding southeast into the bay, and this can be your turnaround point. On your return tip, paddle up into Mowry Canal east of the two spoil islands for a chance to see West Indian manatees at any time of year.

When it's bright, sunny, and calm, the water is very tempting, so if you'd like to take a refreshing swim, paddle out and anchor in deeper water where you feel comfortable swimming.

Alternate route: If you have more time to spend paddling, continue past Fender Point another 2.5 miles to Black Point Park and Marina.

The author's wife paddles along the shoreline of Biscayne Bay near the Biscayne National Park Headquarters at Convoy Point.

Here you can stop in for lunch at the restaurant and maybe even catch one of the local live bands. Portage your canoe or kayak over to the north side of the restaurant so you can keep an eye on it, or use bicycle cable locks to secure it somewhere.

Author's note: There is a canoe-and-kayak launch at Black Point Park and Marina located along the road that accesses the jetty. Be advised that vehicles parked there are commonly vandalized, so after unloading your gear at the launch, it is safer and wiser to move your vehicle to the open parking area nearby and walk back to the launch.

25 Convoy Point to West Arsenicker Key Paddling Route

See map on page 121.

Trailhead GPS coordinates: N25 27' 53.08" / W80 20' 07.77"

Type of trail: Canoeing, kayaking, or paddleboarding

Type of adventure: Paddle over shallow sea-grass beds in Biscayne Bay with opportunities for bird watching, fishing, swimming, and snorkeling.

Total distance: 8.5 miles round-trip

Charts: *Waterproof Top Spot Miami Area Fishing and Diving Recreation Map* (#N211)

Difficulty: Moderate with the possibility of being strenuous if the weather acts up

Time required: Allow for 4 or 5 hours, but take longer if you like.

Special considerations: Always be watchful for thunderstorms and waterspouts.

Scenic value: Outstanding

Overview and Route Description

West Arsenicker Key lies 4.25 miles due south of Convoy Point and is the second largest of the four islands that make up the Arsenicker Keys. These islands got their name from Bahamian settlers who used to raid the heron and egret nests of their eggs for food. The parent birds took exception to their eggs being taken so they would peck at the intruders with their beaks. The term "arsenicker" refers to having your "arse" nicked at by the irate birds. West Arsenicker is the closest key as you paddle south from Convoy Point.

Exactly 2 miles south of Convoy Point, you can't help noticing the Turkey Point Nuclear Power Plant. Do not paddle into the turn basin nor make landfall at the narrow point of land that sticks out into the bay or you will have armed security guards show up in very short order. Turkey Point got its name from the anhinga, a waterbird that was once called a "water turkey" because of its flared tail feathers.

On your way to or from West Arsenicker Key, you will be paddling in water from a few feet deep to about 8 feet deep. If you decide to take a refreshing swim or go snorkeling, simply anchor, raise a dive flag, and hop overboard.

The author on Biscayne Bay with the Arsenicker Keys on the horizon

The species-rich flats around West Arsenicker Key are often alive with sea life, and it is not uncommon to see barracuda, bonefish, very large stingrays, spotted eagle rays, young Atlantic sharp-nosed sharks, nurse sharks, and small bonnethead sharks. Between the Arsenicker Keys and the mangrove-lined mainland, there is a deep channel called Midnight Pass and over the years there have been sightings of hammerhead sharks and tiger sharks in excess of 10 feet long cruising through this pass. Sometimes the sharks swim out of the deep water and up onto the shallow flats in search of rays, which are one of their favorite foods. Once, when a particularly large tiger shark came cruising slowly by me in my kayak with its fins out of the water, I imagined it was thinking, *crunchy on the outside, soft and chewy on the inside*!

As you paddle around these mangrove islands, you can see brown pelicans, egrets, herons, cormorants, and maybe even magnificent frigate birds perched in the trees. In early springtime the Arsenicker Keys come alive with nesting activity, so don't get too close during nesting season because it is illegal and you might even get your arse nicked at by an egret.

26 Convoy Point to Elliott Key Paddling Route

See map on page 121.

Trailhead GPS coordinates: Convoy Point: N25 27' 53.08" / W80 20' 07.77";
Elliott Key marina: N25 27' 12.59" / W80 11' 49.08"

Type of trail: Kayaking or paddleboarding. Canoes are not advised for
crossing the exposed waters of Biscayne Bay unless calm weather conditions
are predicted and, even then, only accomplished canoeists should attempt
this crossing.

Type of adventure: Paddle across open water of Biscayne Bay with the
option of tent camping on Elliott Key. Restrooms are available at the Elliott
Key boat basin.

Total distance: 9.0 miles one-way from Convoy Point to the Elliott Key boat
basin, 18.0 miles round-trip

Charts: *Waterproof Top Spot Miami Area Fishing and Diving Recreation Map*
(#N211)

Difficulty: Moderate to strenuous depending on weather conditions and
tides

Time required: All day or camping overnight on Elliott Key (or Boca Chita
Key)

Special considerations: Check weather reports and always be watchful
for thunderstorms and waterspouts. Be especially cautious of speeding
powerboats in open water—wear bright clothing and fly a colorful flag for
visibility. You will be crossing the Intracoastal Waterway where large boats
often cruise, sometimes at high speed, so be absolutely certain you are
visible. Flying a big American flag should help, but do not fly a dive flag
or a solid red flag because those are nautical flags not to be used while
underway. Summertime mosquitoes on Elliott Key, especially at night,
cannot be described in words, but *horrendous* comes to mind.

Scenic value: Outstanding

Overview and Route Description

For serious paddlers looking for adventure, this can be a very rewarding trip
combined with a good bit of exercise. Camping is available on Elliott Key
if you'd like to spend an evening or two in a tent under the stars, plus there
are some nice hiking trails available on Elliott Key that are fun to explore.
The Elliott Key boat basin also gives you access to Caesar's Creek to the

Brown pelicans nest in mangroves on the islands and shorelines of Biscayne Bay.

south and Sands Cut to the north, both of which lead to the ocean side of the island. There you can paddle over the patch reefs and see a bountiful array of colorful reef fish. Display a dive flag and don your snorkel gear if you'd like. It's like swimming in an aquarium and on clear days the visibility underwater can be 100 feet or more. You can also try your luck fishing.

There is a nature trail that loops from the boat basin to the shoreline along the ocean side and back. The rocky shoreline can be interesting despite all of the trash that gets deposited from tides and ocean currents. Look especially for chitons tightly attached to the shoreline rocks. This mollusk is oblong in outline and dates back 400 million years. Limpets and other mollusks are present as well.

If you paddle around to the rocky, ocean side of Elliott Key, it is often-times choppy with strong tides so be especially cautious if you decide to make landfall. Be advised that tides rip through Caesar's Creek and can be too strong to paddle against. Adventurous kayakers who wish to cir-cumnavigate Elliott Key through Caesar's Creek and Sands Cut will have an 18-mile paddle.

Alternate route: An alternative to camping on Elliott Key is to camp on Boca Chita Key to the north of Elliott Key. It is easily recognizable by the lighthouse on the western side of the island. If you choose this destination, you may want to launch from Black Point Park and Marina 5 miles north of Convoy Point. This places you almost due west of Boca Chita Key and will be a 10-mile paddle across the bay. Leaving from Convoy Point to Boca Chita will be an 11-mile paddle. If you choose to spend some time and camp at both locations, the distance between the Elliott Key and Boca Chita Key boat basins is exactly 5 miles.

Elliott Key is thought by some historians to be named for Andrew Ellicott (1754–1820), who surveyed the eastern coastline of Florida for the US government in the late 1700s and early 1800s. The name "Elliott's Key" appeared sometime after his survey, but if historians are correct, his one chance for fame was dashed by leaving the *c* out of his last name.

Author's note: It is highly advised that paddlers avoid Elliott Key on Columbus Day weekend. This is the weekend of the annual Columbus Day Regatta, which has morphed over the years into an out-of-control party with hundreds of boaters, personal watercraft, and sailboats that gather on the bay side of Elliott Key and far too many drunken partygo-ers. Although it may sound like fun, it would be extremely dangerous for paddlers, and Biscayne National Park brings law-enforcement officers in from many other agencies to keep the event under some semblance of control.

Public Launch Sites for Canoeists and Kayakers that Access Biscayne Bay (south to north)

Homestead Bayfront Park
and Marina
9698 SW 328th St.
Entrance fee. Ramp or shore
launch.

Convoy Point (Biscayne
National Park)
9700 SW 328th St.
Homestead
No fee. Ramp launch.

Black Point Park and Marina
24775 SW 87th Ave.
Miami
Entrance fee. Ramp launch.

Deering Estate at Cutler
16701 SW 72nd Ave.
Cutler Bay
No fee. Ramp or shore launch.

Chapman Field Park
13601 Deering Bay Dr.
Coral Gables
No fee. Ramp launch.

Matheson Hammock Park
9610 Old Cutler Rd.
Coral Gables
Entrance fee. Shore launch.

Hobie Island Beach Park
3301 Rickenbacker Causeway
Virginia Key
No fee. Shore launch.

Crandon Park & Marina
6747 Crandon Blvd.
Key Biscayne
Boat-ramp user fee. Ramp
or shore launch.

Bill Baggs Cape Florida
State Park
1200 Crandon Blvd.
Key Biscayne
Entrance fee. Beach (ocean-
side) or seawall (bay-side)
launch.

Big Cypress National Preserve

Big Cypress National Preserve
Big Cypress Welcome Center
33000 Tamiami Trail East
Ochopee, FL 34141
Phone: (239) 695-4758
Website: nps.gov/bicy

It may seem strange for the general public to learn that in our very midst, we have a tract of land one hundred thirty miles long and seventy miles wide that is as much unknown to the white man as the heart of Africa.

—Hugh L. Willoughby, *Across the Everglades*, 1900

ALTHOUGH THE BIG CYPRESS NATIONAL PRESERVE IS CONTIGUOUS WITH Everglades National Park to the south, it is floristically much different. While the true Everglades are open, watery prairies with a mosaic of hardwood hammocks, pine rocklands, mangroves, and other interrelated ecosystems, the Big Cypress National Preserve is characterized by a more temperate inventory of plants that make up the swamps, hammocks, pinelands, and prairies. Deep cypress sloughs and strands channel water south, and many of these are bisected by Tamiami Trail (US 41). A free brochure map of the preserve that shows the locations of the various sloughs, trails, campsites, and other points of interest is available at the Big Cypress Swamp Welcome Center or the Oasis Visitor Center.

Unlike Everglades National Park, the Big Cypress National Preserve does not have an official entrance, nor is a fee charged to enter the preserve. Big Cypress National Preserve falls under a different management plan than Everglades National Park. The preserve was protected by Congress in 1974 and expanded to 729,000 acres in 1988. Hunting and fishing are allowed, as are all-terrain vehicles (ATVs) and airboats. ATVs, including swamp buggies, are now restricted to designated trails, and permits are

Big Cypress National Preserve Overview

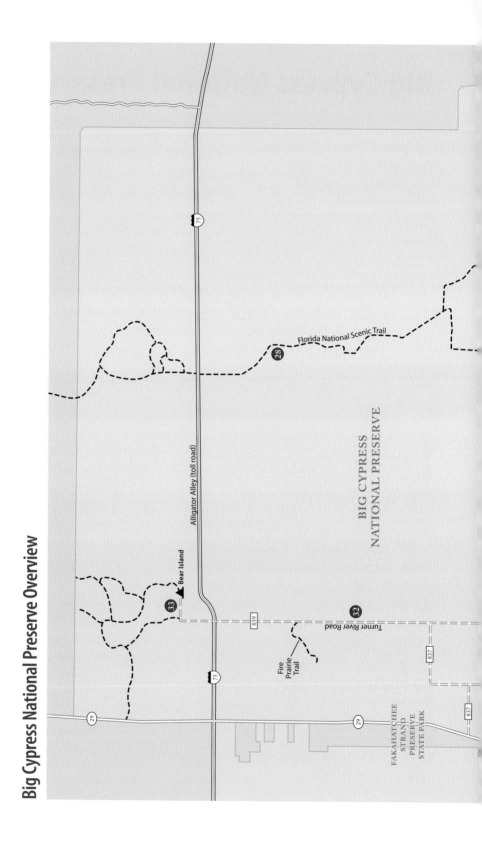

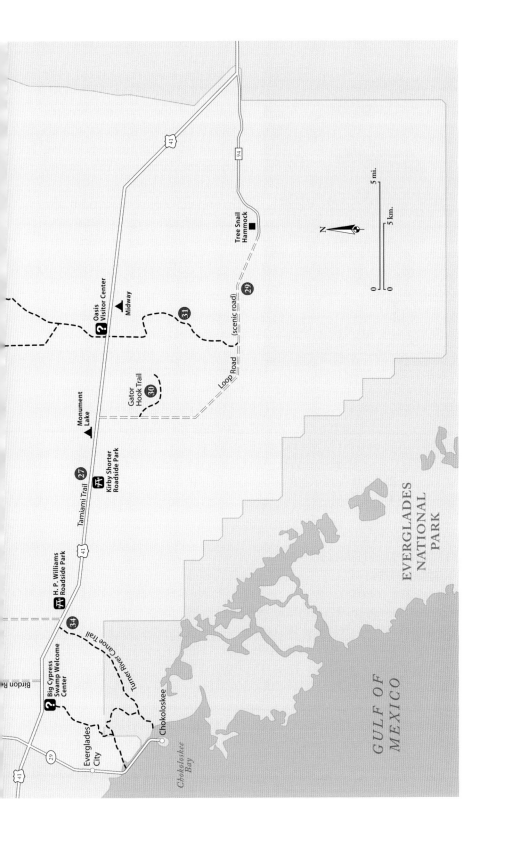

America's national symbol, the bald eagle is a relatively easy bird to see in the Everglades region.

issued by a lottery system. The unregulated use of swamp buggies throughout the years has resulted in many thousands of miles of trails that crisscross the preserve, leaving permanent damage in the form of deep ruts running in all directions. To see the destruction from the air is disheartening. Private land holdings within the preserve also allow hunters the legal right to build cabins and makeshift shelters in remote areas accessible by swamp buggies and other ATVs. The tires of swamp buggies leave deep ruts in the muck that adversely affect the natural water flow and even alter vegetation types. Their banning in parts of the Big Cypress National Preserve has been a contentious issue because of their historical unregulated use.

The Big Cypress Swamp Welcome Center is located about 4 miles west of Turner River Road or 2.8 miles east of SR 29 on the south side of Tamiami Trail (US 41).

Oasis Visitor Center
52105 Tamiami Trail East
Ochopee, FL 34141
Phone: (239) 695-1201
Hours of operation: 8:30 a.m. to 4:30 p.m. daily (closed Dec 25)

The Oasis Visitor Center is located about 55 miles west of Krome Avenue (SW 177th Avenue; SR 997) or 22 miles east of SR 29 along the north side of Tamiami Trail. The Oasis Visitor Center (and the Big Cypress Welcome Center) provides restrooms, a bookstore, exhibits, and an information desk staffed by informative park rangers and volunteers. Be sure to check on scheduled guided tours that may include hikes, swamp walks, or canoe trips. These guided tours are typically offered from

December through April. Outside the visitor centers are opportunities for viewing wildlife around canals. The southern trailhead for hiking the Florida National Scenic Trail is located at the Oasis Visitor Center.

Hunting

Visitors to the Big Cypress National Preserve should be aware of hunting season. During the season always wear blaze-orange hats, shirts, or vests to avoid being mistaken for a deer or other game animal. Check at the visitor centers to learn which areas are safest to explore during hunting season, or to inquire about regulations regarding hunting and fishing in the preserve.

Off-Road Vehicles

Off-road vehicles (ORVs) are allowed by permit within certain designated areas of the Big Cypress National Preserve. ORVs are destructive to plant communities and leave deep, permanent ruts in an otherwise pristine wilderness. ORV owners contend that swamp buggies were historically used to access the interior of the Big Cypress Swamp long before the area became a national preserve in 1974, and they should therefore be allowed. A compromise that restricts ORV use to designated trails is a part of the National Park Service's Recreational Off-Road Vehicle Management Plan.

Safety Hazards

Most of the same safety hazards listed for Everglades National Park apply here as well. Cottonmouth moccasins are rather plentiful in the Big Cypress National Preserve so be especially cautious when exploring watery areas where this venomous snake may occur. In the dry season they aggregate around areas of permanent water in strands, sloughs, alligator holes, and canals. Upland areas may harbor eastern diamondback rattlesnakes and dusky pygmy rattlesnakes. The feral hog is another potentially dangerous animal to be aware of in this region. Although they will almost always run away when humans approach, hogs will defend their young if confronted. These are descendants of free-ranging swine introduced into Florida by Spanish explorers in the sixteenth century. Although they are destructive to natural habitats, they now offer sport for hunters and are a favorite prey of the endangered Florida panther as well.

Venomous snakes, alligators, and other potentially dangerous animals aside, the most hazardous aspect of exploring the Big Cypress National Preserve is driving on Tamiami Trail (US 41). This road is well known to locals as being dangerous due to speeding cars and trucks, so drive extra carefully.

Know the symptoms of heat exhaustion and heatstroke and how to treat these potentially life-threatening health issues. Always bring more water than you think you will need, and always wear sunglasses, a wide-brimmed hat, and lightweight clothing if you are exploring or camping in summer.

Camping

There are eight campgrounds in the Big Cypress National Preserve; five can accommodate RVs and tent campers, and three are available only for tent campers. For campground information the reader is encouraged to visit the Big Cypress National Preserve website (nps.gov/bicy) and go to the camping section for detailed information regarding each site. The campgrounds are Bear Island, Burns Lake, Gator Head, Midway, Mitchell Landing, Monument Lake, Pinecrest, and Pink Jeep. Dispersed backcountry camping is allowed in many areas of the preserve by permit.

A Backcountry Camping Permit is required for all backcountry camping. Permits are free and can be filled out online and printed. Permit forms are also located at every backcountry trailhead and you can get them at both visitor centers. The permits take only a few minutes to complete. See also Backcountry Camping Rules & Regulations on the park website and be sure to let the rangers know that you made it back safely.

Airboats

There are private airboat concessionaires both in and outside of the Miccosukee Indian Reservation along Tamiami Trail, but none are inside the Big Cypress National Preserve. Although airboat rides are popular for tourists, be advised that airboats are loud, disruptive to wildlife, and damaging to any native plants in their path. You will also notice that wild alligators habitually approach commercial airboats when they stop, which is a telltale sign that the alligators are being illegally fed. My personal viewpoint is that ranger-led hikes and canoe trips are far more relaxing and educational ways to see the Big Cypress Swamp than on an airboat.

27 Tamiami Trail Scenic Drive

Trailhead GPS coordinates: East end: N25 45' 42.75" / W80 49' 36.02"; west end: N25 59' 32.20" / W81 35' 23.57"

Type of trail: Sightseeing by automobile with opportunities to stop and explore on foot. Biking is especially dangerous and is definitely not recommended.

Type of adventure: Drive along a designated scenic highway through the Big Cypress National Preserve to Collier-Seminole State Park.

Total distance: 50.0 miles

Charts: Big Cypress brochure map available free at the Big Cypress Welcome Center or the Oasis Visitor Center, or use any Florida road map

Time required: 3 to 4 hours for sightseeing

Special considerations: Dangerously fast traffic so *never* stop in the travel lanes to look at wildlife. If you decide to pull off the roadway, do so on the south side where there is a wide swale. Parking on the north side next to the guardrail is very dangerous. Use your turn signals and allow plenty of time to pull off the road. Also be especially careful when crossing Tamiami Trail on foot, and then always stand on the opposite side of the guardrail between the road and the canal when viewing wildlife.

Scenic value: Excellent. This scenic highway bisects cypress strand and mixed-hardwood swamp habitats that are periodically interrupted by open, sunny prairies.

A menagerie of wading birds gather to feed in shallow water right alongside Tamiami Trail in the Big Cypress National Preserve.

Tamiami Trail Scenic Drive

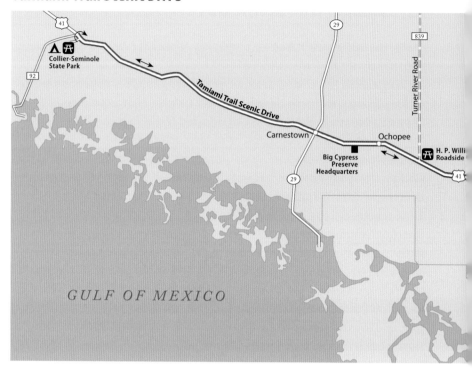

Overview and Route Description

The scenic portion of Tamiami Trail begins in the east at the Forty Mile Bend as you exit the Miccosukee Indian Reservation and continues west through the Big Cypress National Preserve to Collier-Seminole State Park. It is regarded as one of the most scenic highways in Florida. Tamiami Trail was completed in 1928, and its name was taken from the two cities it connects—Tampa and Miami.

An abundance of wildlife, including birds, alligators, otters, snakes, frogs, turtles, and fish, can be seen along this stretch of Tamiami Trail. Even though this is a scenic drive, it cannot be stressed enough that it is also a very dangerous roadway due to trucks and cars that travel at high rates of speed (often well over the posted speed limit). So use extreme caution, do not drive too slowly, and never brake abruptly if you notice wildlife you'd like to stop to see. The wide road swale on the south side of the road is the safest place to stop.

The cypress trees along this route are festooned with bromeliads, including Spanish moss (*Tillandsia usneoides*) that drapes from the tree

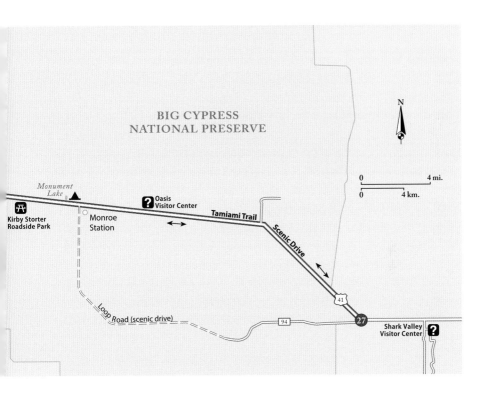

branches. Spanish moss is not a moss, nor is it from Spain. While it is the most widespread of all bromeliads, it is also the most non-bromeliad-looking bromeliad as well. The big clustering bromeliad adorning the trees in mass is the cardinal air plant, or stiff-leaved wild-pine (*Tillandsia fasciculata*). This species produces a branched flower spike covered with red and greenish-yellow bracts. You have to get up close to see the narrow tubular purple flowers hidden among the bracts. Florida is home to sixteen species of native bromeliads, but the most well-known bromeliad in the world is the pineapple.

You will be crossing through the Big Cypress National Preserve so be sure to familiarize yourself with trails in this region. The Kirby Storter Roadside Park, located 7.6 miles west of the Oasis Visitor Center, offers restrooms, picnic tables, and a wheelchair-accessible boardwalk for wildlife viewing. H. P. Williams Roadside Park, located 14.5 miles west of the Oasis Visitor Center, offers restrooms, picnic tables, and a wood boardwalk for viewing wildlife. See also Turner River Road Scenic Drive if you stop at H. P. Williams Roadside Park.

28 Florida National Scenic Trail—Big Cypress

Trailhead GPS coordinates: I-75 rest stop (north): N26 10' 05.47" / W81 04' 31.95"; Oasis Visitor Center (south): N25 51' 24.71" / W81 01' 55.52"

Type of trail: Hiking, backpacking

Type of adventure: Hike or backpack along a marked trail (orange blazes) through prairie, pineland, sloughs, and cypress forests. Members of the Florida Trail Association blaze trees with orange paint to help designate the official trail, but exploring off-trail is allowed. There are side trails blazed with blue that loop off the main trail.

Total distance: Hiking the Florida National Scenic Trail between the Oasis Visitor Center and the rest area along Alligator Alley (I-75; toll road) is 28.0 miles one-way. The Alligator Alley Rest Area is located about 18 miles east of SR 29 for those hiking south to the Oasis Visitor Center or to hike north on the Florida National Scenic Trail (see "Alternate route #2" below). The Roberts Lake Trail can take hikers an additional 8.25 miles south of the Oasis Visitor Center to Loop Road, but this section is no longer a part of the official Florida National Scenic Trail.

Charts: Hikers and backpackers are advised to purchase the Florida Trail Association Map #41–42, which shows this trail (available on the Internet at floridatrail.org or by phoning the Florida Trail Association office in Gainesville, FL, at 352-378-8823). This trail is visible on Google Earth as the Cross Seminole Trail. The Big Cypress brochure map also shows the trail and is available free at the Big Cypress Welcome Center or the Oasis Visitor Center.

Difficulty: Moderate to strenuous; most difficult in summer due to mosquitoes, flooding, oppressive heat, and potentially dangerous lightning storms. Expect muddy areas or standing water, especially during summer and fall.

Time required: Varies; count on 2 to 3 days to complete the trail one-way. There are 2 loop trails blazed with blue that offer shorter hikes (see alternate routes below).

Special considerations: Mosquitoes and biting flies in summer and fall. Remember that you are in a wilderness area that may include encounters with venomous snakes and other wildlife. This portion of the Florida National Scenic Trail is not heavily marked and may become overgrown during the rainy season due to light foot traffic.

Scenic value: Excellent

Overview and Trail Description

First and foremost, the National Park Service strongly encourages hikers to carry a manual compass along with a GPS unit anytime they venture into the Big Cypress backcountry. Do not rely upon a cell phone GPS function because it drains the battery rapidly and may leave hikers without any directional device.

Before beginning your hike, inquire about the trail conditions at the Oasis Visitor Center. Rangers and volunteers at the front desk can answer any pertinent questions and offer firsthand advice. Additional information is available from the Florida Trail Association's website. Bring plenty of water, even if you are only hiking a portion of the trail, and be fully mindful that this is not a trail to underestimate. Although the terrain is mostly flat, this trail is often regarded as one of the most rugged trails to hike in the entire Florida Trail system. Backpacking with a load of camping gear in flooded or muddy conditions can be strenuous, so consider the length of this trail and your skills as a hiker before embarking on your journey. Hikers should anticipate traveling much slower than they are used to in other habitats, with 2 mph being a good pace.

The southern trailhead begins along the raised area adjacent to the airfield north of the Oasis Visitor Center. Once you cross the first prairie, the trail becomes much more scenic as you leave civilization behind. Primitive tent camping is currently available at five designated sites along the trail. The first campsite, called Seven Mile Camp, is 7 miles from the trailhead, and the second campsite, called Ten Mile Camp, is an additional 3-mile hike north. Hike another 7.5 miles and you will reach Thirteen Mile Camp, so named because it's about 13 miles south of I-75.

Continuing north another 5 miles will lead you to the Oak Hill Camp, and by trekking north an additional 4 miles, you will arrive at Ivy Camp. Hiking north from Ivy Camp will lead to the northern trailhead and rest stop along I-75, where the hum of car traffic may be a welcome sound for some but obnoxious to others. The Florida National Scenic Trail continues north more than 900 miles to Escambia County at the western tip of the Florida Panhandle if you have a good pair of hiking shoes and a lot of time to spare.

Wildflowers can be abundant at times, and if you are lucky enough to hike the trail in early summer, you will be rewarded with hundreds of eye-popping pink blossoms of Bartram's rose gentian (*Sabatia decandra*),

Florida National Scenic Trail—Big Cypress

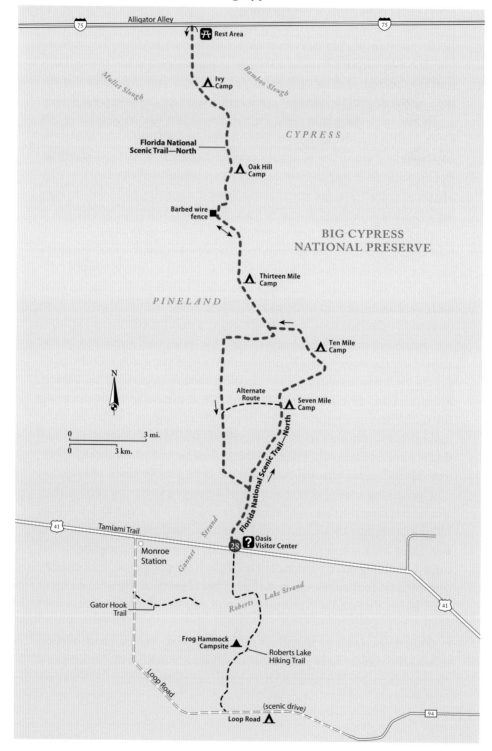

Explorers lucky enough to hike into the vast prairies of the Big Cypress National Preserve in early summer will be greeted by hundreds of blossoms of Bartram's rose gentian.

named to honor the intrepid explorer William Bartram (1739–1823). Bartram traveled through Florida and was the first native-born American to spend his life as a naturalist. His writings about old Florida invoke feelings of envy and gratitude from those of us who grew up here. In early summer you may be lucky enough to see the snowy orchid (*Platanthera nivea*), with glistening white blossoms that smell like grape jam. Look also for the gaudy white flowers of the string lily (*Crinum americanum*) and the alligator lily (*Hymenocallis palmeri*) most any time of year. Sunrises and sunsets are breathtaking.

Alternate route #1: There is an alternate route for hikers beginning at the Oasis Visitor Center who do not wish to thru-hike this trail. From the Oasis Ranger Station, hike north on the orange-blazed trail to an intersection on your left marked with blue blazes. Follow the blue-blazed trail back to the orange trail to the west, turn left, and return to the Oasis Visitor Center. This will be a nice half-day hike.

Alternate route #2: There is a second alternate route from the rest area off Alligator Alley (I-75) that offers half-day, full-day, or overnight options. From the rest area, hike north beneath the I-75 overpass to the trailhead on the east end of the cleared area. The trail leads north to a 14-mile loop with two cross trails that offer shorter loops. There are five campsites along this loop trail, which are shown on the Big Cypress brochure map. The west side of the trail is blazed orange because it is a part of the official Florida National Scenic Trail. If you are not thru-hiking the trail, take the blue trail to the right. The shortest loop will be to take the red-blazed trail to the left, the next shortest will be the yellow-blazed trail to the left, and the longer loop will be to stay on the blue-blazed trail back to the orange trail and then turn south to complete the loop. If you do decide to take the Florida National Scenic Trail north of this loop, you will need official permission to enter the Seminole Indian Reservation. Contact the Florida Trail Association for further information.

Note: The Big Cypress and Alligator Amblers chapters of the Florida Trail Association help maintain the Big Cypress National Preserve portion of the Florida National Scenic Trail. Hikers are encouraged to contact these chapters for more detailed information or to join in on one of their hikes through the region. If you meet up with any of them on the trail, thank them for their dedication and hard work.

About the Florida Trail Association and the Florida National Scenic Trail

Members of the Florida Trail Association, which currently has eighteen chapters throughout Florida, help maintain the Florida National Scenic Trail. Each chapter holds monthly meetings for fellowship and educational programs and to plan and coordinate group-sponsored hikes, paddling trips, and trail-maintenance activities. If you are new to Florida and wish to learn more about areas to hike, bike, or paddle, the Florida Trail Association is a rewarding outlet for information and camaraderie. For detailed information visit their website at floridatrail.org or phone (352) 378-8823. You can also e-mail them at fta@floridatrail.org.

If you like chatting with other hiking enthusiasts, you may wish to register on the whiteblaze.net forum, which is a community of Appalachian Trail disciples from Florida to Maine. The forum features help topics, trail news and updates, articles, member trip reports, a forum for female hikers, campsites, health and safety information, and more.

Although you do not need to be a member of the Florida Trail Association to hike along the Florida National Scenic Trail, portions of the trail lead through private property and membership is a legal requirement to cross these private land holdings.

The entire Florida National Scenic Trail is 1,300 miles long, but this may change from year to year as members and volunteers work to move portions of the trail off private lands and away from roadways by relocating it through publicly owned natural corridors as they become available. Check the Florida Trail Association's website for "Notices to Hikers," or subscribe to their online mailing list for updated information on routes and access.

The Florida Trail Association offers an End-to-End certificate and patch for members who complete the entire Florida National Scenic Trail. To qualify, you must hike the entire trail as it exists at the time of your hike, and this includes portions of the trail along roadways (no hitchhiking!).

(continued on next page)

At least thirty days before departure, you are required to notify the Florida Trail Association of your intent to thru-hike. You must supply the association with such information as an address, phone number, emergency contact, and your proposed day-to-day itinerary. This is required because the Florida Trail Association must notify private-land owners of the date and time hikers are expected to cross their property (private-land owners may change their access policies at any time). As a courtesy to future hikers, respect private and public property at all times. You will be crossing portions of the Seminole Indian Reservation and federal property (Eglin Air Force Base), so you must have a letter with you from the Florida Trail Association in case you are stopped and questioned. Permits are required for portions of the trail—check out the Florida Trail Association's website under National Scenic Trail / Permits. Be sure you acquire all of the pertinent maps and read *Florida Trail Companion Guide for Long Distance Hikers*, available from the Florida Trail Association. The book contains information on campsites, water sources, nearby towns, post offices, and other valuable information. Maps of the Florida National Scenic Trail are available at the Florida Trail Association's main office in Gainesville or through the Florida Trail Association's online store at floridatrail.org. Happy hiking!

29 Loop Road Scenic Drive

Trailhead GPS coordinates: East entrance: N25 45' 42.85" / W80 49' 38.58"; west entrance: N25 51' 48.93" / W81 06' 02.03"
Type of trail: Scenic driving or biking
Type of adventure: Sightsee by vehicle or bicycle on a road that is paved on the east end for 8 miles and gravel the remainder of the way, with opportunities to stop and explore on foot.
Total distance: 24.0 miles between entrances on Tamiami Trail
Charts: Big Cypress brochure map available free at the Big Cypress Welcome Center or the Oasis Visitor Center
Difficulty: Easy to moderate on a bicycle
Time required: 1 hour or more in a vehicle; all day on a bicycle
Special considerations: Occasional potholes in the road. Mosquitoes and biting flies can be problems in summer and fall if you are on a bicycle. There are no gas stations, food stores, or restroom facilities along Loop Road.
Scenic value: Excellent. Loop Road traverses cypress and mixed-hardwood swamp habitat.

Overview and Route Description

Loop Road (CR 94) can be accessed by driving 3.8 miles west of Shark Valley on Tamiami Trail (US 41) to the Forty Mile Bend (take the left exit where Tamiami Trail turns northwest). The Tamiami Ranger Station is located at the turnoff. For those traveling east on Tamiami Trail, turn south at Monroe Station to access Loop Road.

There are opportunities to see white-tailed deer, black bears, river otters, feral hogs, and even endangered Florida panthers on or near the road (a good reason to drive slowly). The small village of Pinecrest offers a glimpse of home life for some very hardy people who got tired of city life and moved to this remote area to take up residence. Imagine living where the nearest town with a grocery store is more than an hour's drive in either direction. It is definitely a no-frills lifestyle, but the people who chose it wouldn't give it up for anything. The eastern portion is now lined with homes built by Miccosukee Indians complete with satellite dishes and other modern amenities.

There is primitive group camping available at the Pinecrest campsite (6 miles west of the eastern entrance to Loop Road off Tamiami Trail;

Loop Road Scenic Drive

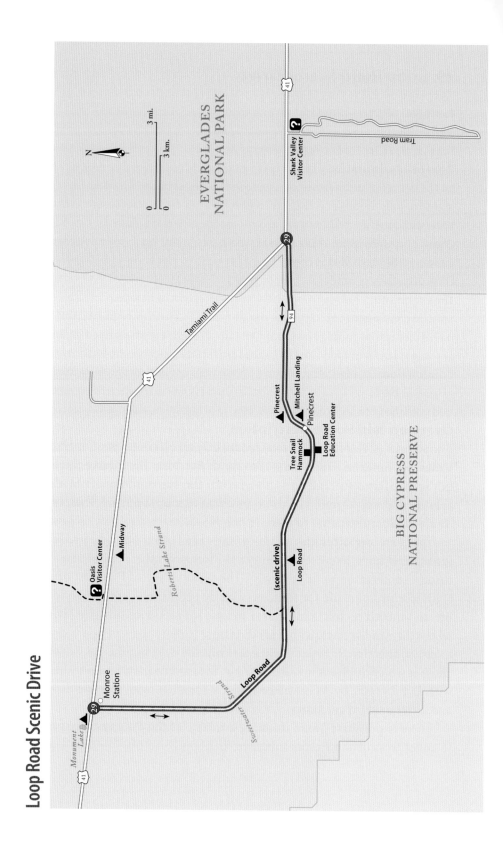

reservations required). This campsite is on the north side of Loop Road. The Mitchell Landing campsite is 1 mile farther west on the south side of Loop Road. Two miles farther west is the Loop Road Education Center (about 9 miles west of Tamiami Trail), where there is a short hiking trail on the north side of Loop Road that is worth exploring. It is called the Tree Snail Hammock Trail.

Watch for interesting birds—especially limpkins—while driving slowly along Loop Road, and keep an eye out for snakes, turtles, frogs, and other critters on the road or in the adjacent canal along parts of the drive. The southern terminus of the Roberts Lake Trail can be accessed off Loop Road as well. Take note that if you are traveling east to west on Loop Road, you will bypass the Oasis Visitor Center. If you want to visit the center after your Loop Road tour, you will have to drive east about 4 miles once you get back on Tamiami Trail.

Be sure to stop at Sweetwater Strand near the western end of Loop Road. It is marked with signage and often has wading birds, alligators, and the occasional family of river otters.

Loop Road was once a wild and lawless place where society's outcasts and misfits went to hide from the law or to escape society itself. Back in the day, an old, wooden saloon called the Gator Hook was tucked away 5 miles east of Tamiami Trail in the swampy recesses of Loop Road and it was one rough place. So rough, it is said, that when two young teenage boys approached the front door one evening, a man out front asked what they were doing there. When one of the boys said they'd just like to go inside, the man asked if they were armed. When they politely answered "no sir," the man suggested that they go back home and fetch a gun or a knife. The Gator Hook closed in the 1970s, which was probably a good thing.

30 Gator Hook Trail

Trailhead GPS coordinates: N25 49' 53.61" / W81 06' 01.72"

Type of trail: Hiking. Bicycles are not advised because of numerous exposed cypress knees and roots on the trail as well as muddy and flooded conditions most of the year.

Type of adventure: Hike along a marked trail (yellow blazes) through cypress and Everglades prairie habitats with opportunities to explore deep cypress domes.

Total distance: 4.8 miles round-trip

Charts: Florida Trails Association Map #42 shows the trail as a dotted line. The trail is also visible on Google Earth, and it is shown on the Big Cypress National Preserve brochure map without much detail.

Difficulty: Moderate

Time required: 2 hours round-trip

Special considerations: Uneven terrain coupled with mud and standing water up to knee-deep on parts of the trail. Watch for cottonmouth moccasins and diamondback rattlesnakes, plus alligators in the deeper water inside cypress domes. As a precaution, place valuables inside the trunk of your car.

Scenic value: Outstanding, especially inside the cypress domes. A great trail to hike out on for sunsets.

Overview and Route Description

This is a relatively new trail that offers a very scenic hike through freshwater wetland habitats with side trails that lead to nearby cypress domes. When exploring cypress domes, be especially aware of cottonmouth moccasins and large alligators, and keep track of where the main trail is located. The trail is marked with signage and there are two picnic shelters, an information kiosk, and restrooms available at the parking area. The beginning of the trail is elevated, with numerous cypress knees and exposed roots, before becoming muddy and then flooded, so do not wear your best shoes. Water socks or sneakers are good, or even going barefoot is an option, although that creates an easier chance of being bitten by venomous snakes.

In summertime there is a water-lily-like plant in the cypress domes called floating hearts (*Nymphoides aquatia*) that produces small, attractive, white flowers that dot the water surface. Look also for yellow flowers protruding

Gator Hook Trail

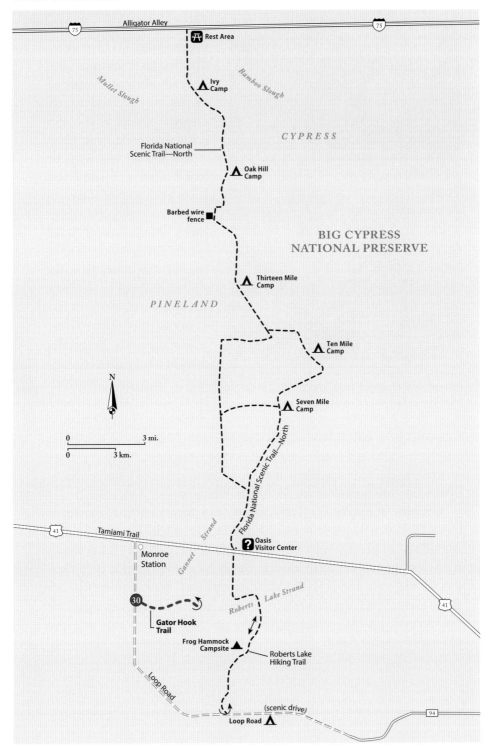

Alligator Alley

75

Rest Area

Mullet Slough

Bamboo Slough

Ivy Camp

CYPRESS

Florida National
Scenic Trail—North

Oak Hill
Camp

Barbed wire
fence

BIG CYPRESS
NATIONAL PRESERVE

Thirteen Mile
Camp

PINELAND

Ten Mile
Camp

N

Seven Mile
Camp

0   3 mi.
0   3 km.

Florida National Scenic Trail—North

Strand

Tamiami Trail

41

Gannet

Monroe
Station

Oasis
Visitor Center

Roberts Lake Strand

30

Gator Hook
Trail

Roberts

41

Frog Hammock
Campsite

Roberts Lake
Hiking Trail

Loop Road

(scenic drive)

94

Loop Road

Although cardinal air plants are very common on cypress trees along the Gator Hook Trail, they are a state-listed endangered species.

from the water, which belong to carnivorous plants called bladderworts (*Utricularia*) that entrap microorganisms in small bladders connected to the leaves. Another carnivorous species in the area is the small butterwort (*Pinguicula pumila*), which can be found growing in damp soil. It has a tiny rosette of greasy-feeling leaves with small blue, violet, or pink flowers. Small insects (especially ants) become trapped on the leaves and are digested by enzymes. Another interesting wildflower in this region is the yellow, daisy-like Everglades daisy or southeastern sneezeweed (*Helenium pinnatifidum*). Look for it especially in winter and spring when it forms fields of yellow beneath the cypress trees. Members of this genus have been dried and used as snuff by Native Americans, hence the name sneezeweed. Interesting, too, is that the genus *Helenium* honors Helen of Troy, whose abduction started the Trojan War.

Growing as epiphytes on the cypress trees are a number of species of bromeliads, but the most noticeable species is the stiff-leaved wild-pine or cardinal air plant (*Tillandsia fasciculata*). When in flower it has showy red bracts that encase small, tubular, purple blossoms. It forms large clusters on the trees and is visible all along the trail. There is plenty to see along Gator Hook Trail so take your time. Binoculars and a compass are recommended. If you somehow lose the trail, heading due west will lead you back to Loop Road.

31 Roberts Lake Hiking Trail

Trailhead GPS coordinates: North trailhead: N25 51' 23.62" / W81 01' 55.77"; south trailhead: N25 48' 13.68" / W81 01' 14.72"

Type of trail: Hiking, backpacking

Type of adventure: Hike along a marked trail (blue blazes) through freshwater wetlands of the Big Cypress Swamp.

Total distance: 16.5 miles round-trip

Charts: Hikers and backpackers are advised to purchase the Florida Trail Association Map #4142, which shows this trail (available on the Internet at floridatrail.org or by phoning the Florida Trail Association office in Gainesville, FL, at 352-378-8823). Due to tree canopy, parts of this trail are not visible on Google Earth.

Difficulty: Moderate to strenuous

Time required: All day to complete the trail round-trip in the winter dry season. During the wet season it is best to plan a one-direction trip or hike for awhile and turn around.

Special considerations: Mosquitoes and biting flies in summer and fall. Uneven trail can be slippery when muddy or flooded. Bring a hiking pole for support. Eastern diamondback rattlesnakes and cottonmouth moccasins are possibilities so be aware. Alligators may occur in areas of deeper water.

Scenic value: Excellent. This is a scenic trail that is seldom traveled. If you are looking for solitude in a pristine area with good bird-watching opportunities, then this trail is a gem.

Overview and Route Description

The trail was named for Roberts Lake Strand, which drains into Gator Hook Swamp and is one of the most scenic cypress strands in the Big Cypress National Preserve. The north trailhead is located directly across Tamiami Trail (US 41) from the Oasis Visitor Center and terminates at Loop Road 8.25 miles to the south. (*Option*: If you choose to start on Loop Road and hike north to the Oasis Visitor Center, the southern trailhead is marked by a blue blaze. Note that part of this trail on Google Earth is indicated as the Cross Seminole Trail. There are no designated parking areas or restroom facilities at the southern trailhead. Unless you have two vehicles for transportation from one end back to the other, it is advised that you hike from the northern trailhead at Oasis south to Roberts Lake Strand and then hike back.)

Roberts Lake Hiking Trail

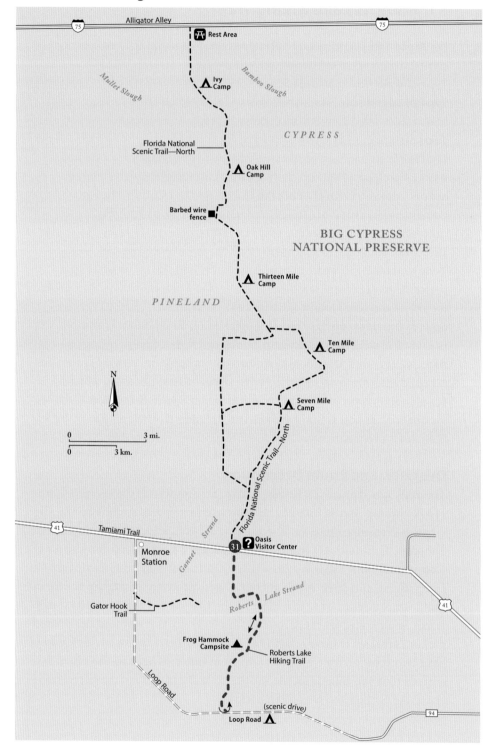

It is easier to hike this trail during the dry season, but the word "dry" in the Everglades region is relative because you still might be slogging through water even in the winter dry season. Actually, it is more interesting and refreshing to hike when the trail is flooded. Water levels may range from ankle- to knee-deep, unless you decide to sidetrack into one of the deep sloughs, where the water may be waist-deep or more. At one point this trail joins up with the Gator Hook Trail, which could offer an alternative route back to the westernmost north–south portion of Loop Road, but this juncture is not at all obvious and should only be attempted by wilderness-savvy hikers. If you misjudge the juncture and end up lost, simply continue hiking due west until you emerge on Loop Road. Hike north on Loop Road to Tamiami Trail, and the Oasis Visitor Center will then be about 4 miles to the east. At the intersection of Loop Road and Tamiami Trail is an old, now-dilapidated wood building called Monroe Station, which was once a lively hangout for hunters and locals, but it closed in the 1990s.

Take your time and look for unusual epiphytes (ferns, bromeliads, orchids) growing on the trees, a variety of birds, and even the occasional mammal, reptile, or amphibian to make your hike interesting and memorable. If you find that you have lost the trail (or it lost you), use your compass or GPS to continue on a due north or south heading (depending, of course, on which direction you are hiking). North leads you back to Tamiami Trail and south will take you to Loop Road. Cell phone coverage is spotty at best here.

Endangered Florida panthers frequent this area, so even a fleeting glimpse of this secretive predator will be one of those special moments that will linger in your mind for a lifetime. Bobcats, river otters, feral hogs, white-tailed deer, and Florida black bears are possible to see as well.

For backpackers the Frog Hammock Campsite is located 3.3 miles from the trailhead at Loop Road or about 5.0 miles south of the Oasis Visitor Center. It is well marked. As a precaution against vandalism, if you plan on camping overnight, it is advisable that you hike north to south so you can leave your vehicle at the Oasis Visitor Center instead of along desolate Loop Road.

This trail is no longer a part of the official Florida National Scenic Trail so my best advice is to check with the rangers and volunteers at the Oasis Visitor Center to inquire about trail conditions and other details.

32 Turner River Road Scenic Drive

Trailhead GPS coordinates: N25 53' 16.12" / W81 15' 45.14"

Type of trail: Scenic driving or biking. Hiking is OK also but it is a long, straight, dirt road.

Type of adventure: Drive or bike along a graded dirt road that bisects a variety of habitats, including mixed-hardwood forests, cypress strands, prairies, and pineland. A canal borders the road on the east side.

Total distance: 20.0 miles one-way

Charts: Big Cypress brochure map available at the Oasis Visitor Center or Big Cypress Visitor Center

Difficulty: Easy to moderate, depending on your mode of travel

Time required: 2 hours by car, all day by bicycle

Special considerations: The road is very dusty during the dry season and there may be occasional potholes. Proceed slowly and with caution. Be courteous and slow down when approaching parked vehicles and people, especially when the roadway is dusty. There are private land holdings along this road as well, so please respect private property.

Scenic value: Excellent. This can be a very rewarding sightseeing trip. Some of the views are outstanding, and wildlife abounds in and around the canal during most of the year. It is best during low water when wildlife congregates around deeper, and more permanent, water sources.

Overview and Route Description

Turner River Road (CR 839) begins at the H. P. Williams Roadside Park along Tamiami Trail (US 41). It terminates 20 miles to the north at the Bear Island Unit of Big Cypress National Preserve just past the I-75 overpass (no access).

Sightseeing from your car with periodic stops along the way is a popular venue for those who drive this road. The canal that borders the road can be lively with alligators, otters, wading birds, ducks, and sometimes hundreds of swallows that swarm down en masse to sip water on the wing. Drive slowly to avoid running over snakes, turtles, and other wildlife that cross the road.

If there is a hard rain that floods parts of the road, don't be surprised to see walking catfish hobbling on their fins from one side of the road to the other. Wild populations of this Asian catfish are a result of the

Turner River Road Scenic Drive

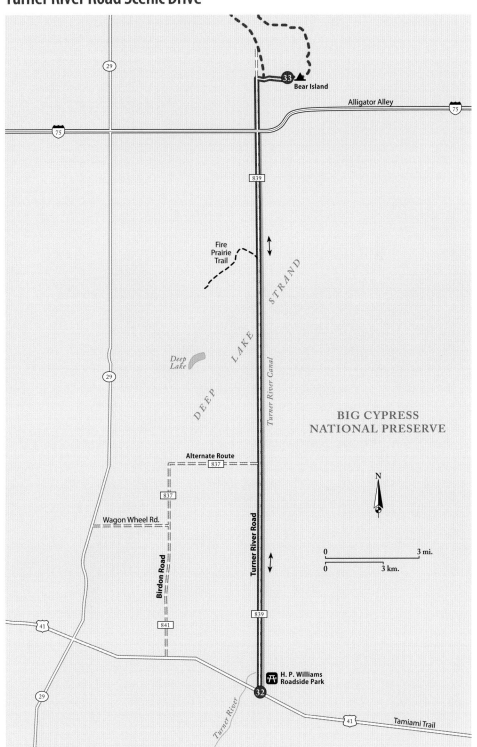

aquarium trade and are now well established in man-made canals and natural waterways throughout much of the Everglades region. To see a fish crossing a road is a bizarre sight.

Turner River Road can also be a great adventure for biking enthusiasts, but parts of the road can be rough (sometimes like a washboard) if it has not been graded recently, and it can be very dusty in the dry season when cars pass by, so take this into consideration. The same goes for hikers.

Alternate route: Turner River Road bisects with Wagon Wheel Road and offers a 16.6-mile loop back to Tamiami Trail via Birdon Road (CR 841). From the H. P. Williams Roadside Park, take Turner River Road north 7.3 miles to Upper Wagon Wheel Road (CR 837). Turn left and proceed 3.0 miles west to the south turn. At 2.0 miles south, Lower Wagon Wheel Road turns west to SR 29, but continue south 6.3 miles on Birdon Road to Tamiami Trail.

The canal alongside Turner River Road is one of the best places in the Everglades region to be able to view wildlife right from your car or bicycle.

33 Bear Island Trails

If you are looking for out-of-the-way adventure, consider the Bear Island Unit of the Big Cypress National Preserve for hiking, biking, and primitive camping.

See map on page 159.

Trailhead GPS coordinates: N26 10' 51.87" / W81 14' 20.82"

Type of trail: Hiking or biking

Type of adventure: Hike or bike on trails that traverse upland and wetland habitats. Camp in designated campsites with nearby restroom facilities.

Total distance: More than 20 miles of trail available

Charts: The Big Cypress National Preserve brochure map shows the area, but consult Google Earth for the best detail. You can also find a map of the trails at nps.gov/bicy/planyourvisit.

Difficulty: Easy to moderate

Time required: Plan on at least 2 hours

Special considerations: Mosquitoes and biting flies in summer and fall. Hunters and off-road vehicles during hunting season.

Scenic value: Excellent. These trails cross through pristine native habitats and offer scenic vistas, bird-watching opportunities, and an abundance of native wildflowers.

Overview and Route Description

The Bear Island Unit is accessible off the Turner River Road 20 miles north of Tamiami Trail. Drive north on Turner River Road 18.4 miles from Tamiami Trail to the I-75 overpass (no access from Turner River Road) and proceed another 1.6 miles to a turnoff to the east. Drive east about 1.8 miles to an open parking area on the right. Camping is now by reservation only and campsites are nothing more than open, cleared ground. There are restrooms available near the camping areas. During hunting season there is a manned wildlife check station on your way in and out of the Bear Island Unit. If you plan on hiking or biking the trails during hunting season, be sure to wear something bright orange as a safety precaution. Reflective orange vests are a good idea.

The main trail leads north from the parking area and continues for many miles. One loop trail for cyclists or intrepid hikers is 13 miles long and can be seen by zooming in on the area using Google Earth. Most visitors hike along the trail and then turn around and return the same way they hiked in. Some of the interesting animals that live in this region are Florida panthers, Florida black bears, white-tailed deer, feral hogs, river otters, hispid cotton rats, raccoons, opossums, eastern gray squirrels, fox squirrels, and Southern flying squirrels. Birds abound and there is a chance to see red-cockaded woodpeckers, pileated woodpeckers, brown-headed nuthatches, eastern bluebirds, wild turkeys, swallow-tailed kites, barred owls, great horned owls, and a host of other species. American robins are common in winter, along with other migratory species.

Wild pennyroyal leaves emit a strong minty fragrance when crushed. It is common along the Bear Island Trails.

If you're lucky enough to be in this region in April or May, the many-flowered grass-pink (*Calopogon multiflorus*) can be found here if a fire has burned through the habitat the previous year. This beautiful terrestrial orchid is on the southern edge of its range in the Bear Island Unit. There are also such interesting species as southern dewberry (*Rubus trivialis*), shiny blueberry (*Vaccinium myrsinites*), wild pennyroyal (*Piloblephis rigida*), and long-lipped ladies' tresses (*Spiranthes longilabris*). A real rarity to be found in this region is the Fakahatchee burmannia (*Burmannia flava*). If you're a butterfly enthusiast, keep your eye out for zebra swallowtails, palamedes swallowtails, viceroys, and other interesting species, including a host of skippers. If you decide to explore off the trails, be cautious of eastern diamondback rattlesnakes in upland areas and cottonmouth moccasins around depression marshes. And, speaking of wet areas, some trails in the Bear Island Unit can be flooded during the rainy season.

34 Turner River and Halfway Creek Paddling Trails

Trailhead GPS coordinates: Turner River: N25 53' 30.17" / W81 16' 15.47";
Halfway Creek: N25 53' 32.41" / W81 19' 35.58"
Type of trail: Canoeing or kayaking
Type of adventure: Canoe or kayak along mangrove-lined creeks with the
option of paddling to Chokoloskee Bay, Chokoloskee Island, Everglades City,
or the Ten Thousand Islands.
Total distance: 8.0 miles from the Turner River trailhead to Chokoloskee
Island; about 6 miles from the Halfway Creek trailhead to the Chokoloskee
causeway or to the Gulf Coast Visitor Center
Charts: NOAA Chart #11430 (Lostmans River to Wiggins Pass); Waterproof
Chart #41 (Everglades & Ten Thousand Islands), although the scale on the
waterproof chart is too small to be of much use for navigation; *National
Geographic Trails Illustrated Map #243: Everglades National Park* shows these
trails but is not very detailed.
Difficulty: Moderate to difficult, depending on weather conditions and tides
Time required: 5 to 6 hours or more
Special considerations: Mosquitoes and biting flies in summer and fall.
Tides and wind can make paddling a strenuous ordeal at times, especially in
the open waters of Chokoloskee Bay. Parts of these trails may be impassable
during low tide in the dry season. The Turner River can become overly
popular in the busy tourist season in winter, so paddlers wanting more
solitude might consider Halfway Creek instead. How full the parking lot is
will be a good indication.
Scenic value: Good to excellent. The Turner River meanders through
freshwater marsh and mangrove habitat, and Halfway Creek traverses
mangrove habitat. Both trails are scenic and offer access to the Ten Thousand
Islands and Chokoloskee Island.

Overview and Route Description

These trails are combined because they connect to each other and the
trailheads are only about 3.5 miles apart. The Turner River Canoe Trail
is located at a new parking area on the north side of Tamiami Trail (US
41) and is marked with signage. Here is where paddlers can offload their
canoes or kayaks and leave their vehicles (restrooms available). The first
section of Turner River is relatively straight and begins in a beautiful

Turner River and Halfway Creek Paddling Trails

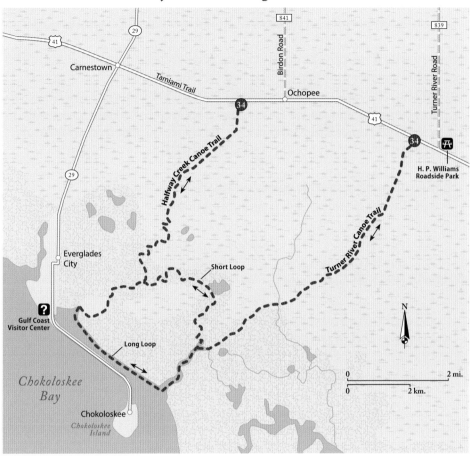

freshwater marsh before becoming brackish mangrove habitat. If you have two vehicles, you can leave one at the Halfway Creek trailhead, which will allow your party to paddle a 13- to 14-mile loop or a 16- to 17-mile loop by connecting the two trails.

The turnoff to the right after paddling 6 miles along the Turner River is the shorter route. This creek is shaped like an upside down U and will lead you to Halfway Creek; turn right and the creek will terminate at the Halfway Creek trailhead near Seagrape Drive. A longer loop is possible by continuing along the Turner River Trail to Chokoloskee Bay, turning right and hugging the shoreline until you reach the entrance back into

Halfway Creek, and then turning right (north) into the creek. Be advised that the last option requires you to paddle 2.5 miles in an open bay. If winds are strong, especially from the west or southwest, conditions can be rough.

The trailhead for the Halfway Creek Canoe Trail is along Seagrape Drive at the Big Cypress Welcome Center located 2.25 miles east of the Tamiami Trail and SR 29 intersection. Again, this trail can be looped back to the Turner River Trail or it can be a one-way trail that terminates either at the causeway leading to Chokoloskee Island or at the boat ramp near the Gulf Coast Visitor Center. There are shuttle services in Everglades City that can reunite you and your gear with your vehicle.

Both of these trails can be impassable in the dry season, especially at a low tide around a full or new moon. It is advisable to check with the rangers at the Gulf Coast Visitor Center in Everglades National Park or at the Big Cypress Welcome Center, either in person or in advance by phone, to see if these trails are passable.

Fakahatchee Strand Preserve State Park

Fakahatchee Strand Preserve State Park
137 Coast Line Dr.
Copeland, FL 34137
Phone: (239) 695-4593
Website: floridastateparks.org/fakahatcheestrand

You would have to want something very badly to go looking for it in the Fakahatchee Strand.

> —Susan Orlean, from "A Green Hell,"
> *The Book of the Everglades*, 2002

THE ENTRANCE TO THE 82,000-ACRE FAKAHATCHEE STRAND PRESERVE State Park is located 2.5 miles north of Tamiami Trail (US 41) on SR 29. Turn west at the sign for W. J. Janes Memorial Scenic Drive (CR 837 West), and then turn right to reach the ranger station a short distance north on your right. Janes Memorial Scenic Drive is 11 miles one-way and is a narrow, graded, dirt road that is closed to vehicle traffic from sunset to 8 a.m. daily. It is, indeed, a scenic drive, but if you do nothing more than drive its length, you will have missed the opportunity to see firsthand one of the real gems of the award-winning Florida state park system. If you are looking for real wild Florida, this is it.

The Fakahatchee Strand was logged into the 1950s, and a complex network of elevated tram roads crisscross the swamp. These were built to allow trunks of ancient cypress trees to be hauled out of the swamp by narrow-gauge trains. Fortunately for the state of Florida—its residents, visitors, wildlife, and rare flora—the Fakahatchee Strand was purchased for preservation in 1974, the same year the Big Cypress Swamp became a national preserve. The Fakahatchee Strand is a linear drainage system that channels freshwater from the Okaloacoochee Slough into the Ten

Fakahatchee Strand Preserve State Park Overview Map

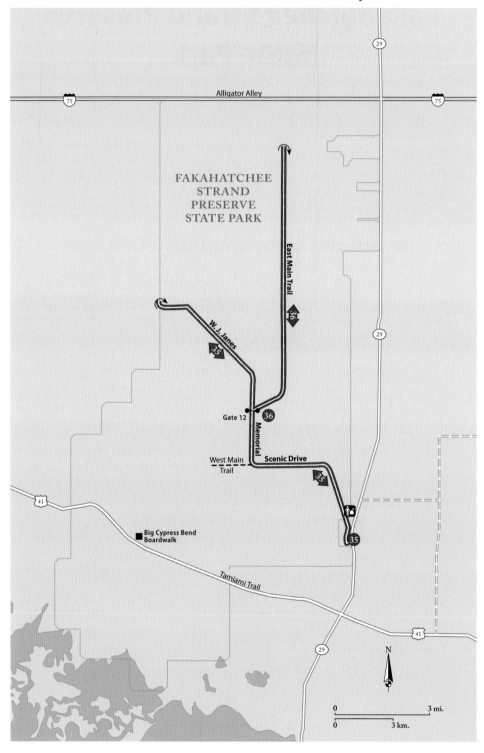

Thousand Islands region along the Gulf of Mexico. It is literally a forested river during the rainy season.

Some of the old tram roads have been cleared and offer comparatively easy access into the interior of the swamp. Botanically, this swamp is the crown jewel of Florida. Impressive numbers of native orchids, ferns, and bromeliads grace the swamp, and some are among the rarest plants in Florida. A few of the extremely rare species are the moss orchid (*Cranichis muscosa*), tall neottia (*Cyclopogon elatus*), hanging club moss (*Huperzia dichotoma*), tiny orchid (*Lepanthopsis melanantha*), hatchet orchid (*Pelexia adnata*), dwarf butterfly orchid (*Prosthechea pygmaea*), and stately maiden fern (*Thelypteris grandis*). Some are terrestrial, growing in the ground like normal plants, but many are epiphytic, adapted to growing on trees to gain access to better light conditions and to take advantage of a niche not available to other plants. Some trees are veritable air gardens of epiphytic plants.

The Fakahatchee Swamp is not only botanically rich, it is home to many rare animals as well. Here your footprints can mingle with those of Florida panthers, Florida black bears, and Everglades mink. All three of these animals occasionally can be sighted crossing Janes Memorial Scenic Drive, the main road leading through the preserve. Springtime is the best season to see Everglades mink—they resemble small weasels with a loping gait. They are voracious hunters that eat crayfish, snakes, and amphibians, but they also attack marsh rabbits and other mammals that outweigh them. If you should see one cross the road while driving, biking, or hiking, stop and be perfectly quiet and it may likely come back out. Florida panthers are rarely seen and many sightings turn out to be the smaller and less timid bobcat. Florida panthers are tawny colored with a long tail, unlike the bobcat, which is smaller and has a stubby tail. Keep a watchful eye out for them walking on, or across, Janes Scenic Drive.

Birdlife in the Fakahatchee Swamp is exceptional, so be sure to bring binoculars. Here you can see common resident birds along with a wide array of rare or migratory species. During the late winter and spring dry season, fish become concentrated in deeper areas, such as roadside canals, and this bounty of food attracts wading birds such as herons, egrets, and wood storks that show up in large numbers to take advantage of the feeding opportunity. Colorful wood ducks and purple gallinules also frequent the canal along Janes Scenic Drive. Travel slowly so you don't

The deep sloughs in the interior of the Fakahatchee Strand in Collier County are among the prettiest and most botanically interesting habitats in Florida.

miss anything and out of courtesy to wildlife that may dart across the road. Don't let a road-killed animal be a memory of your visit.

Also be aware that cottonmouth moccasins are abundant in the Fakahatchee Swamp so it is wise to step with caution, most especially if you are traveling off-trail in the interior of the swamp. Cottonmouth moccasins do not attack people, as is often claimed, but they are belligerent and typically hold their ground when approached. When threatened the cottonmouth moccasin will fling its mouth open to reveal the white inner lining, a polite warning worth heeding. They are well camouflaged so pay very close attention to your immediate surroundings.

The Fakahatchee Swamp was almost turned into a household word by Susan Orlean in her bestselling book *The Orchid Thief*. It is a true story of a man named John LaRoche who was caught stealing orchids, including the famed ghost orchid (*Dendrophylax lindenii*). He was with several Seminole Indians and his claim was that they had the right as Native Americans to take whatever plants they wanted, but a judge disagreed, fining both LaRoche and the Seminoles. The book led to the movie *Adaptation*, starring Meryl Streep and Nicolas Cage, about the trials and tribulations involved in making the book into a movie. The movie, of course, was filled with intrigue, drama, and aphrodisiac-induced wild sex.

Due to orchid poaching, some sloughs within the Fakahatchee Swamp are now closely monitored with hidden, motion-detecting cameras. The same goes with parking areas along Janes Scenic Drive.

Guided Walks:
Friends of Fakahatchee
605 Webb Rd.
Everglades City, FL 34139
Phone: (239) 695-1023
Website: orchidswamp.org

Friends of Fakahatchee volunteers offer 2.5-hour tram rides along Janes Scenic Memorial Drive as well as swamp walks for adventurous travelers. The popular Moonlit Tram Tours at night sell out quickly. Friends of Fakahatchee volunteers are dedicated to supporting and preserving the Fakahatchee Strand Preserve State Park by educating the public about its importance. To help support Friends of Fakahatchee by making a donation, sign up for a swamp walk, or jump onboard the Ghost Rider tram; either phone their office in Everglades City or visit their website and click on "Tours and Events" in the upper right corner of their home page. You can sign up by clicking on the tour of your choice.

35 W. J. Janes Memorial Scenic Drive

Winfred J. Janes was a Collier County commissioner who, in 1962, was the driving force behind the appropriation of $30,000 to conduct a feasibility study to build Alligator Alley (I-75) through the Everglades and connect Broward County with Florida's west coast. The Associated Press referred to it as "the most controversial road ever built in Florida." W. J. Janes Memorial Scenic Drive is 11 miles of graded dirt road that cuts through the Fakahatchee Strand, offering motorists, hikers, and bikers an opportunity to view all sorts of wildlife without having to actually wallow around in a foreboding swamp. You can stop and take a swamp tromp off-trail if you'd like, but proceed with due caution and use every bit of common sense you can muster because this is a swamp with real dangers, the least of which is getting lost.

There is one parking area along Janes Drive at the trailhead of East Main, an elevated tram road that is kept cleared by park rangers and volunteers working for a group called Friends of Fakahatchee. If you would prefer a 2.5-hour guided tram ride along Janes Scenic Drive, check at the ranger station or visit orchidswamp.org. Advance reservations are required.

See map on page 168.

Trailhead GPS coordinates: N25 56' 44.01" / W81 21' 28.92"

Type of trail: Graded dirt road

Type of adventure: Scenic driving, hiking, or biking

Total distance: 22.0 miles round-trip if you drive or bike the full distance

Difficulty: Easy to moderate for bikers and hikers. Off-trail hiking can be strenuous.

Time required: At least 2 or 3 hours just to get the feel of the place. Spend the day if you like.

Special considerations: For hikers there may be large alligators, cottonmouth moccasins, eastern diamondback rattlesnakes, and dusky pygmy rattlesnakes sunning on, or crawling across, the roads and trails. Give them a respectful berth. Mosquitoes and biting flies can be bothersome in summer, but they're generally at tolerable levels. Avoid heat exhaustion by drinking plenty of fluids.

Scenic value: Outstanding. This is real wild Florida, not a theme park.

Overview and Route Description

Along Janes Scenic Drive there are opportunities to see white-tailed deer, Florida panthers, Florida black bears, Everglades mink, river otters, American alligators, feral hogs, and a wide variety of snakes, turtles, frogs, lizards, and birds. It really is a scenic drive so take your time and see what sort of nature is put on display for your viewing enjoyment.

Janes Drive eventually leads to a maze of crisscrossing roads left over from a failed development project. It is not wise to continue farther because many roads dead-end and leave you wondering if you will ever emerge from the maze. One road does lead to I-75, but lucky is the person who finds it. It's best to drive along Janes Scenic Drive and then turn around once you decide it's time. Mountain bikes or hybrids are recommended for this road.

36 East Main Trail (Gate 12)

See map on page 168.
Trailhead GPS coordinates: N26 00' 27.58" / W81 24' 40.18"
Type of trail: Hiking or biking
Type of adventure: Hike or bike along a historic tram road that bisects a mature hardwood swamp.
Total distance: 6.0 miles round-trip
Difficulty: Moderate, either hiking or biking
Time required: Allow for several hours to take in the scenery.
Special considerations: Alligators and venomous snakes (mostly cottonmouth moccasins) should be watched for and avoided. Alligators are mostly in the canals adjacent to tram roads and in the interior lakes; cottonmouth moccasins are scattered throughout the preserve. Mosquitoes and biting flies can be bothersome in summer and early fall. Off-trail exploring in the interior of the preserve can be strenuous and often requires wading in knee- to waist-deep water (or deeper). Sunken logs can bruise shins, so jeans are recommended. Carrying a compass or GPS is highly advised.
Scenic value: Outstanding. This is one of the most picturesque preserves in Florida, although there are those who may find it hard to envision a swamp as being picturesque. Few people get to see the deep and foreboding interior of the swamp, but some of the deep sloughs are fascinating and intriguing. No matter how one feels about swamps, to explore the Fakahatchee is one of those memories that will remain with you for a lifetime.

Overview and Route Description

The trailhead is located about 6.5 miles north of the ranger station on W. J. Janes Memorial Scenic Drive. It is marked by parking areas on both sides of the road. The East Main Trail entrance is at the north end of the east parking area.

Even though the swamp was plundered for its lumber, it has recovered to the point where it is difficult for anyone to imagine the onslaught that once took place. The swamp appears to be pristine to the casual observer, but the network of tram roads that extend the entire 20-mile length of the swamp and the thousands of cypress stumps scattered throughout the interior attest to the pillage. But all of those cypress stumps have now

The endangered ghost orchid was made famous by the bestselling book The Orchid Thief *and grows wild only in southwestern Florida and Cuba. It blooms at the height of mosquito season in the summer.*

transformed into prime habitat for ferns and terrestrial orchids and are also convenient lounging places for fat cottonmouth moccasins. Another distinctive feature of this swamp is the presence of royal palms (*Roystonea regia*) that tower well above the other trees. These stately and majestic Florida native palms are commonly seen as street trees along roadways of southern and central Florida.

Off-trail exploring is allowed in the preserve but use your best common sense. A manual compass is a must and a handheld GPS unit is a bonus. Do not rely upon cell phone service as a safety net, and be absolutely certain to let the park rangers know your travel plans and what time you expect to return. Remember that Janes Memorial Scenic Drive closes at dusk.

Alternate route: There is another trail, known as the West Main Trail, for which the trailhead is located 4.5 miles from the ranger station on Janes Scenic Drive. From the ranger station drive northeast to the turn that leads due west. The trail begins right where the road makes the next sharp turn to the north. This trail terminates at an open prairie 3 miles from the trailhead and can be hiked or biked. You return the same way you went in. For cyclists, mountain bikes are recommended for this trail.

About the Florida Panther

The Florida panther (*Felis concolor coryi*) is so rare that it is on the federal endangered-species list. Other names are puma and cougar. Males weigh up to 160 pounds and females may reach 100 pounds. Both sexes are tawny above and white below and have a long tail with a crook on the end. To set the record straight, black (melanistic) Florida panthers are nonexistent and any reports of these mythical animals can be attributed to Florida black bears, Labrador retrievers, poor lighting, or way too much whiskey.

The critically endangered Florida panther is a secretive, seldom-seen cat that now exists in only a tiny remnant of its historic range, centered in southwest Florida.

The total number of Florida panthers is now estimated to be fewer than 160 individuals, and highway collisions account for more deaths than any other source, although habitat destruction is the biggest threat to all of Florida's wildlife. The Florida panther is currently known to be in four southern Florida counties: Collier, Glades, Hendry, and Miami-Dade, with most of them residing in and around the Fakahatchee Swamp and the Bear Island Unit of the Big Cypress Swamp, both in Collier County. They feed mostly on mammals, and their diet typically includes white-tailed deer, feral hogs, raccoons, opossum, and armadillos. Birds, alligators, and snakes are also on their menu.

Most of the wild Florida panthers are collared with radio-telemetry devices to track their movements or to find them should they die, either from natural causes or as a road kill, so drive with care in panther habitat. If you should see one of these magnificent cats, consider yourself extremely fortunate.

Collier-Seminole State Park

Collier-Seminole State Park
20200 East Tamiami Trail
Naples, FL 34114
Phone: (239) 394-3397
Website: floridastateparks.org/park/Collier-Seminole

Collier-Seminole State Park is open daily from 8 a.m. to 7:30 p.m. in summer and from 8 a.m. to 5:30 p.m. in winter. The park offers opportunities for boating, camping, canoeing, kayaking, hiking, biking, fishing, photography, wildlife viewing, picnicking, geocaching, and canoe rentals. The park encompasses 7,271 acres, with more than half of the acreage designated as wilderness areas. There is a backcountry campsite, which can accommodate up to six campers, available by permit to paddlers.

Entrance Fee

There is a small fee per vehicle with up to eight passengers and for walk-in or bike-in visitors.

Camping

Tent and recreational vehicle (RV) camping is available on a first-come, first-served basis, or you can make prior reservations. To make reservations, phone Reserve America toll-free at (800) 326-3521, visit reserveamerica .com, or visit floridastateparks.org. Reservations can be made up to eleven months in advance of your visit, but be advised that your credit card is charged at the time the reservation is made and there is a cancellation fee should you change your plans.

Collier-Seminole State Park Overview

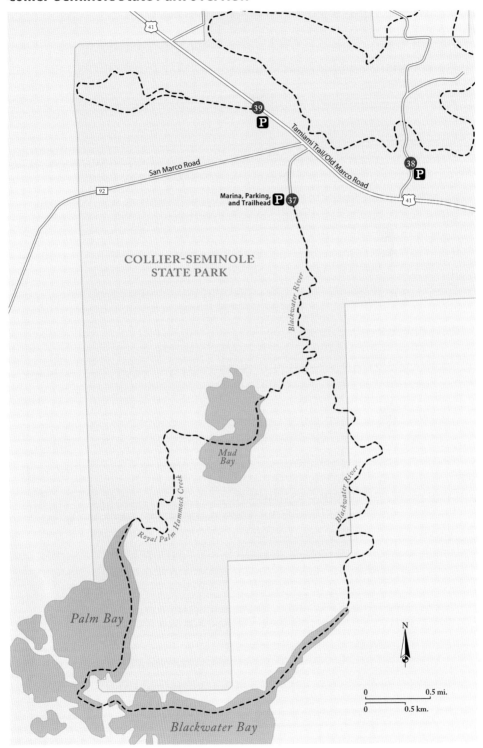

37 Marco Blackwater River Paddling Trail

Trailhead GPS coordinates: N25 59' 16.75" / W81 35' 39.39"

Type of trail: Canoeing or kayaking (powerboats can traverse the Blackwater River portion of the trail)

Type of adventure: Paddle through bays and estuarine tidal creeks that traverse mangrove habitat.

Total distance: 13.5-mile loop

Charts: NOAA Chart #11430 (Lostmans River to Wiggins Pass) or Waterproof Chart #41 (Everglades & Ten Thousand Islands). There is a free park map available from the ranger station that shows the entire loop as well.

Difficulty: Moderate to strenuous depending on tides and wind conditions

Time required: All day, so leave early if you plan on completing the entire loop. Paddlers are required to report back to the ranger station by 5 p.m. during summer hours, and by 4 p.m. during winter hours.

Special considerations: Mosquitoes and biting flies in summer and fall. Tides can be strong and wind can be a concern in open bays. Check with park rangers for tidal conditions because Mud Bay can be impassable at low tide, especially near full- and new-moon phases. Pets are not allowed in rental canoes. It is not advisable to bring pets along in private canoes either because dogs may attract the attention of large alligators.

Scenic value: Excellent. There are scenic views along tidal creeks and across open bays with opportunities to view birds, American alligators, American crocodiles, West Indian manatees, bottlenose dolphins, ospreys, bald eagles, and other wildlife of the region.

Overview and Route Description

The trailhead is located inside the park at the surface ramp along the Blackwater River. You must register at the ranger station before you launch, and you must have all required safety equipment (one life jacket per person; whistle; flashlight). Canoe rentals are available from a concessionaire inside the park, but you must have your own canoe or kayak if you plan to camp in the backcountry. Canoe rentals come with one life jacket per person, one flotation device (throwable cushion) per canoe, and one paddle per person.

The Marco Blackwater River Canoe Trail traverses a designated wilderness preserve. In order to maintain its scenic value, there are very few

Marco Blackwater River Paddling Trail

Egrets, roseate spoonbills, and white ibis take flight along the Blackwater River.

markers along the western portions of the trail between Palm Bay and Marker 47 located along Blackwater River. Be advised that powerboats can access the Blackwater River from either inside the park or from areas outside the park. Primitive tent camping is available at the Grocery Place campsite located between Palm Bay and Mud Bay. To access this camp-site from the Blackwater River without completing the entire loop, turn right into the creek at Marker 47, assuming the tide is high enough to allow passage across Mud Bay. This shallow bay will be impassable at low tide, especially on or near a full- or new-moon phase, so timing is every-thing. Check tide phases before leaving.

There are ample fishing opportunities in this area, and fish to target are spotted sea trout, snook, redfish, mangrove snapper, black drum, and sheepshead. Be sure to check on license requirements as well as fishing regulations and restrictions before wetting a line.

Now-extinct Calusa Indians once inhabited this region. When you are paddling along the rivers and creeks, you are exploring the same areas they traversed in dugout canoes more than 300 years ago.

38 Collier-Seminole Hiking Adventure Trail

Trailhead GPS coordinates: N25 59' 16.11" / W81 34' 46.86"
Type of trail: Hiking or backpacking
Type of adventure: Hike or backpack along a blazed trail through mixed-hardwood swamp, cypress strand, and other scenic habitats, with the option to camp at a primitive campsite.
Total distance: 6.5 miles to complete the loop, but a shorter, 3.0-mile loop is also available from the same trailhead by taking a service road back to the trailhead
Difficulty: Moderate to strenuous depending on conditions
Charts: A free map of the trail is available at the ranger station. The trail is hidden by trees so Google Earth is not helpful.
Time required: 3 to 4 hours to enjoy the entire loop
Special considerations: Mosquitoes and biting flies in summer and fall. Some portions of the trail may be flooded to waist-deep during the rainy season, so this is not a trail for small children or inexperienced hikers. No potable water or facilities along the trail. A hiking pole is helpful on flooded trails to help maintain balance (a broom or mop handle is sufficient).
Scenic value: Excellent. A portion of this trail leads through a mixed-hardwood swamp with native royal palms towering above the forest.

Overview and Route Description

The trailhead is located about 0.75 mile east of the park entrance on the north side of Tamiami Trail/Old Marco Road (US 41) and is indicated by an opening in the guard rail with a narrow, gravel road.

Note: Before hiking or backpacking on this trail, you must go to the ranger station to register and receive the trail gate combination to access the parking area. Bring a fully charged cell phone and the park office number in the event you should get lost or have a medical emergency.

Orange blazes on the trees help designate this rugged trail for hikers. Florida panthers, Florida black bears, bobcats, deer, and other mammals inhabit this region, so if you find any muddy areas, look for their tracks. Panthers and bears typically avoid humans so consider yourself lucky if you see them. During the proper season some interesting wildflowers viewable from this trail include the coastal rose gentian (*Sabatia calycina*), the incredibly showy Bartram's rose gentian (*Sabatia decandra*),

Collier-Seminole Hiking Adventure Trail; Collier-Seminole Mountain Bike and Hiking Trail

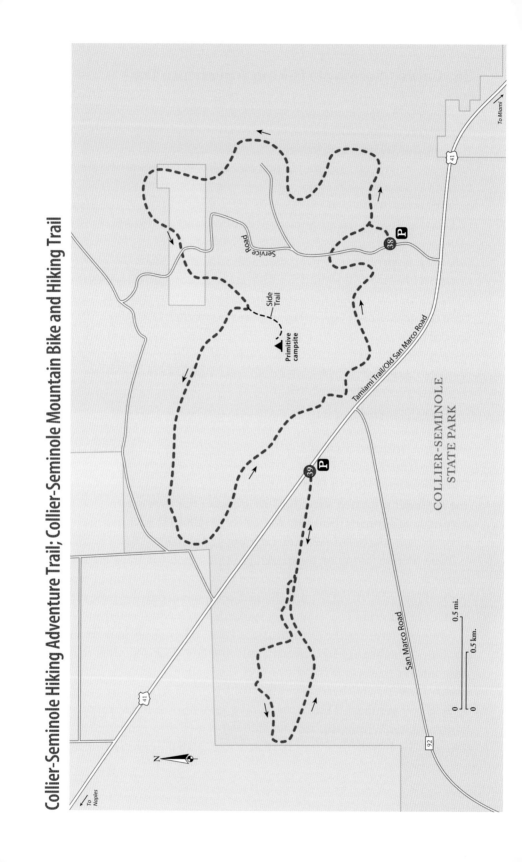

the threatened and fragrant snowy orchid (*Platanthera nivea*), Chapman's goldenrod (*Solidago odora* var. *chapmanii*), and a host of other interesting species, including towering royal palms (*Roystonea regia*) and giant leather ferns (*Acrostichum danaeifolium*).

Bring binoculars because there are ample opportunities for birding as well as butterfly and dragonfly watching. Look for birds of prey, including hawks, falcons, bald eagles, swallow-tailed kites, and ospreys, soaring overhead. The area can be particularly active with warblers during spring and fall migration. American robins can be common in winter.

The backpacker's campsite is located in a dry oak hammock at the terminus of a short side trail that leads south and then west into the interior of the loop. Portable camp stoves are recommended for cooking, and campers are advised to secure their food at night from raccoons or possibly even black bears. Pets, horses, bicycles, and off-road vehicles are prohibited. Campfires are allowed in designated sites. This trail is called the Collier-Seminole Hiking Trail on the Florida Trail Association website (floridatrail.org).

39 Collier-Seminole Mountain Bike and Hiking Trail

See map on page 184.
Trailhead GPS coordinates: N25 59' 54.54" / W81 35' 54.28"
Type of trail: Hiking or biking
Type of adventure: Hike or bike along an elevated loop trail through pine flatwoods and freshwater marsh habitat. Mountain bikes are recommended.
Total distance: 3.5 miles round-trip
Charts: A free map of the trail is available at the ranger station. Portions of the trail are visible on Google Earth.
Difficulty: Easy to moderate
Time required: Allow for 2 hours on foot or 1 hour by bike.
Special considerations: Mosquitoes and biting flies in summer and fall. Park at the trailhead to avoid biking or hiking along Tamiami Trail from the main park entrance.
Scenic value: Excellent. This is a nice trail to hike or bike while viewing birds and other wildlife, as well as native flowering plants.

Overview and Route Description

The trailhead is located 0.75 mile west of the park entrance along Tamiami Trail/Old Marco Road (US 41) and is indicated by a parking area and signage. Walk around the gate at the parking area and make a right turn around a chain about 50 yards down Old Marco Road. From there continue south along Old Marco Road about a mile, then take the trail to the right at the bridge. This begins a loop trail and is advertised by the park as a great trail for cyclists and avid hikers. It will eventually reach a road bordered by a canal, so take a left and follow it about 200 yards where it intersects with Old Marco Road. Turn left and continue your trip back to the trailhead. This is an excellent, dry trail for spending some time, so hike or bike slowly so you won't miss a photo opportunity. There are opportunities to see alligators along this trail.

The butterfly orchid is Florida's most common epiphytic orchid and can be found in mangrove swamps, hardwood forests, and cypress swamps. It flowers in summer.

Corkscrew Swamp Sanctuary and Blair Audubon Center

Corkscrew Swamp Sanctuary and Blair Audubon Center
375 Sanctuary Rd. West
Naples, FL 34120
Office phone: (239) 348-9151
Website: corkscrew.audubon.org

CORKSCREW SWAMP IS THE PREMIER NATIONAL AUDUBON SOCIETY sanctuary in the United States. This is a must-see destination if you have an interest in Florida's flora and fauna—especially birds. And the good news is that you can quietly explore more than 2 miles of swamp on an elevated boardwalk without ever getting your feet wet and muddy. The boardwalk begins and ends at the Blair Audubon Center, where visitors can receive firsthand information about the sanctuary from very informative volunteers and Audubon employees at the front desk. Inside the Blair Audubon Center is the Nature Store, which offers an impressive array of books, videos, clothing, binoculars, cameras, bird feeders, birdhouses, jewelry, an assortment of games and toys for children of all ages, and much more. There are even soothing music CDs along with recordings of Florida birdsongs for your listening and learning enjoyment.

Also located inside the Blair Audubon Center are the Swamp Senses Media Theater, restrooms, classrooms, a photo gallery, and a food service that offers cold sandwiches, drinks, and snacks that can either be eaten there or enjoyed outdoors in the front picnic area. Along the back of the Blair Audubon Center is a covered porch with benches and comfortable rocking chairs to relax in, and these are perfect locations to watch the bird feeders. These feeders attract such birds as painted buntings, indigo buntings, sparrows, woodpeckers, cardinals, blue jays, and many other resident and seasonal species, viewable right from your rocking chair! The sanctuary is also prime habitat for Florida panthers, Florida black bears, white-tailed deer, and other wildlife. This is Old Florida so don't miss it!

Corkscrew Swamp Sanctuary and Blair Audubon Center

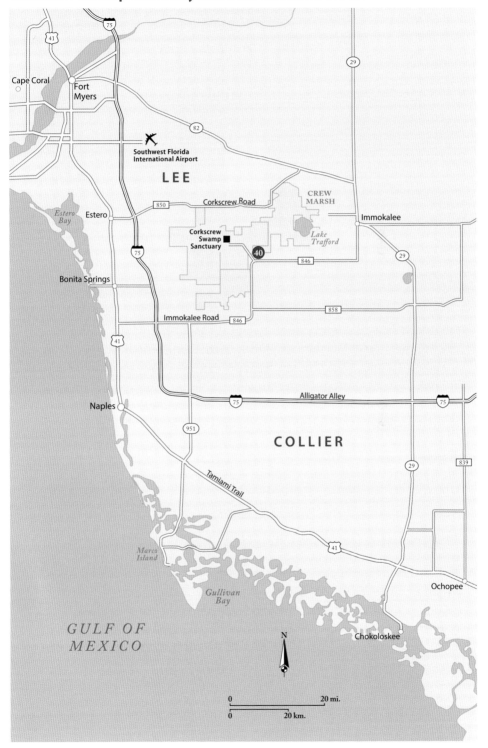

Ruby-throated hummingbirds migrate to South Florida in the fall and remain there until they fly back north to their breeding grounds in the spring.

Fees

Current fees for admission are listed on the Corkscrew Swamp website (corkscrew.audubon.org) or you can inquire by telephone.

National Audubon Society Membership

National Audubon Society members receive a discount to enter Corkscrew Swamp Sanctuary. By joining the National Audubon Society, you also become a member of your state and local Audubon chapters along with receiving *Audubon* magazine each month. To become a member, inquire in the Blair Audubon Center at Corkscrew Swamp Sanctuary or visit the National Audubon Society's website at audubon.org.

40 Corkscrew Swamp Sanctuary Boardwalk

See map on page 189.
Trailhead GPS coordinates: N26 22' 32.53" / W81 36' 13.18"
Type of trail: Walking
Type of adventure: Walk along an elevated boardwalk and view an abundance of birdlife, along with other wildlife, in their natural habitat.
Total distance: 2.25-mile loop or a shorter 1-mile loop
Difficulty: Easy. Wheelchair accessible.
Time required: 3 hours or more to fully enjoy what the swamp has to offer
Special considerations: Mosquitoes never seem to be very bothersome because of the slow-moving water and an abundance of mosquito fish (*Gambusia*) that eat them in their larval stage.
Scenic value: Outstanding. This elevated boardwalk offers extraordinary scenic views of what wild Florida looked like before much of it was lost to development, agriculture, and theme parks.

Overview and Route Description

The trail begins directly outside of the Blair Audubon Center with an elevated boardwalk that leads visitors through pine flatwoods, cypress and mixed-hardwood swamp, wet prairies, and sloughs that make up the 13,000-acre preserve. The entire boardwalk is more than 2 miles in length, and there are covered pavilions and sitting areas along the way to either relax in or escape a rainstorm. There is a 1-mile loop that allows for a shorter excursion.

Corkscrew Swamp is extraordinarily wild and beautiful, but it is the birdlife that attracts many thousands of visitors to this special place each year. A great variety of birds are visible from the boardwalk, and the surrounding swamp is a preeminent wood stork rookery. The best times to see wood stork nesting activities are late winter and early spring. Dedicated and informed volunteers are often stationed along the boardwalk in strategic locations to help point out some of the hidden secrets that the casual visitor might not see. Barred owls are often visible in daytime, and volunteers may have spotting scopes trained on them for visitors to stop and take a closer look. There is much to see, so this is definitely not a place for a hurried visit. Seasoned and amateur birders alike will find this to be one of the most rewarding and memorable places to visit in all of Florida.

The storied ghost orchid (*Dendrophylax lindenii*) is here as well, and one such famous plant grows high up on a cypress tree, sometimes producing a dozen or more blossoms at a time. When in flower you can see it from the boardwalk with binoculars or through spotting scopes trained on it by volunteer staff.

In open areas of the swamp are two species of native hibiscus. The scarlet rose mallow (*Hibiscus coccineus*) produces showy, brilliant red blossoms in late spring and early summer and has palmate leaves that closely resemble marijuana, so don't think you've discovered someone's stash. The swamp rose mallow (*Hibiscus grandiflorus*) has extravagant pink flowers that make their debut in springtime. Bromeliads abound in the trees, and the most common species, the cardinal air plant or stiff-leaved wild-pine (*Tillandsia fasciculata*), forms large clusters of urn-like plants with branched spikes of showy red-and-yellow bracts. If you're lucky, you might get to see ruby-throated hummingbirds sipping nectar from the tubular purple flowers, which are almost hidden by the bracts.

Walk slowly, stop often, and listen attentively for the sounds of nature, like the loud calls and hammering of pileated woodpeckers, the melodious cacophony of frogs and toads, or the mournful wails of the limpkin. Growling alligators and grunting pig frogs add to the symphony.

Birders migrate here in flocks, and some will be dressed as if they are heading out on a weeklong African safari. If they are bent on seeing some rare bird out along the boardwalk, it's best to step out of their way.

Male painted buntings are one of the most spectacular songbirds in North America. They migrate to South Florida in fall and stay through spring, so look for them in the feeders at Corkscrew Swamp from October to May.

CREW Marsh (Corkscrew Regional Ecosystem Watershed)

CREW Marsh (Corkscrew Regional Ecosystem Watershed)
4600 Corkscrew Rd.
Immokalee, FL 34142
Main office: (239) 657-2253; crewtrust.org

THE CREW ACQUISITION PROJECT IS A 60,000-ACRE WATERSHED WEST of the town of Immokalee. Relatively few people know of this preserve, much less enjoy the miles of trails available to hikers, bikers, and geocache enthusiasts. This is surprising because the site surrounds the popular Corkscrew Swamp Sanctuary, which welcomes many thousands of visitors yearly. The hiking trails at CREW Marsh are well maintained, but some portions of the trails may be flooded during the rainy season, so prepare to wade if you're hiking during the rainy season.

Camping

There are two primitive campsites available at the CREW Marsh for individuals and groups. To access the campsites at CREW Marsh or Cypress Dome Trails, campers will be given vehicle access through Gate 3 after obtaining a Special Use Permit. Dogs are allowed on a leash.

To camp, you will need to apply for a Special Use Permit available online at crewtrust.org. At the menu for Site Location, choose either CREW Marsh Campsite Gate 3 or CREW Cypress Dome Trails Campsite Gate 5. The system is fully automated and will only take a few minutes to process. To view your Special Use Permit, you must have the latest version of Adobe Acrobat Reader installed on your computer. There are no restroom facilities at the campsites and no running water so prepare accordingly. Printable maps of the campsites are on the website, and please note the phone number to call if you need to cancel your reservation.

CREW Marsh (Corkscrew Regional Ecosystem Watershed)

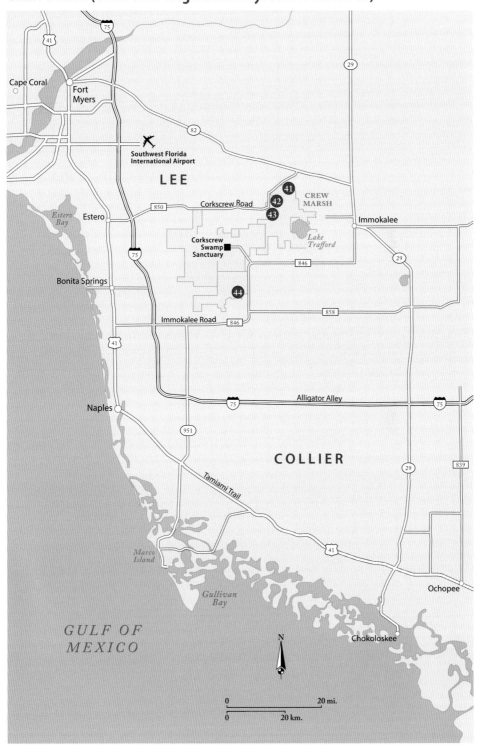

Brochures and trail maps are available at the kiosk near the trailheads or they can be printed off the website in advance of your visit. There are a number of loop trails available that traverse habitats ranging from freshwater marsh, pine flatwoods, and oak hammock to pop ash sloughs, and these trails can be very interesting during all seasons. The site includes the Pine Flatwoods Trail, Hammock Trail, Pop Ash Slough Trail, Marsh Loop Trail, and the Alternative Marsh Trail. All of the trails eventually connect to one another, so it's easy to pick and choose the distance you wish to travel.

There are currently more than fifty geocaches hidden near the CREW trail system and more than thirty can be found at the Bird Rookery Swamp Trails. With the coordinates and a GPS, you can go on your own private treasure hunt. Caches sometimes get relocated or swapped out so check the website often. For more information on geocaching go to geocaching.com.

41 CREW Marsh Hiking Trails (Gate 1)

From Tamiami Trail (US 41) turn north on SR 29 and proceed north through the city of Immokalee. About 5 miles past the city limits, turn left (west) on SR 82. Drive west a few miles to CR 850 (Corkscrew Road) and turn left (south). The CREW Marsh Trail entrance is 1.5 miles south on your left and is marked with signage.

From I-75 take exit 123 and proceed east on Corkscrew Road (CR 850). Drive about 18 miles and the entrance is on your right.

Trailhead GPS coordinates: N26 29' 31.43" / W81 32' 02.38"

Type of trail: Hiking, geocaching

Type of adventure: Hike along marked loop trails through pine flatwoods, freshwater marsh, and mesic oak hammocks.

Total distance: Round-trip from the trailhead: Pine Flatwoods Trail 1.5 miles; Marsh Trail 1.85 miles; Pop Ash Slough Trail 1.5 miles; Marsh Loop Trail 1.5 miles; Hammock Trail 2.5 miles

Charts: Use the brochure map available at the trailhead kiosk.

Difficulty: Easy to moderate

Time required: Allow for 2 hours, but it's easy to spend a half day or more on the trails.

Special considerations: Mosquitoes and biting flies in summer and fall, but they are usually at tolerable levels. Ticks and chiggers can be present in the dry season. Eastern diamondback rattlesnakes are present so be safe and stay alert. Also stay alert for black bears and feral hogs.

Scenic value: Excellent. This is a nice sandy trail to hike while viewing birds and other wildlife, as well as native flowering plants. There is a possibility to see Florida panthers, Florida black bears, bobcats, feral hogs, wild turkeys, and other interesting fauna. Wildflowers abound.

Overview and Route Description

The CREW Marsh Hiking Trails are a well-kept secret so enjoy the peace and solitude. For wildflower enthusiasts the CREW Marsh represents the southern edge of the natural range of many species of native wildflowers due to the sandy habitat that is not found south of this region. Here you can find such species as the endemic Florida scrub roseling (*Callisia ornata*), coastal plain honeycombhead (*Balduina angustifolia*), and pine barren frostweed (*Crocanthemum corymbosum*), none of which occur in

CREW Marsh Hiking Trails (Gate 1)

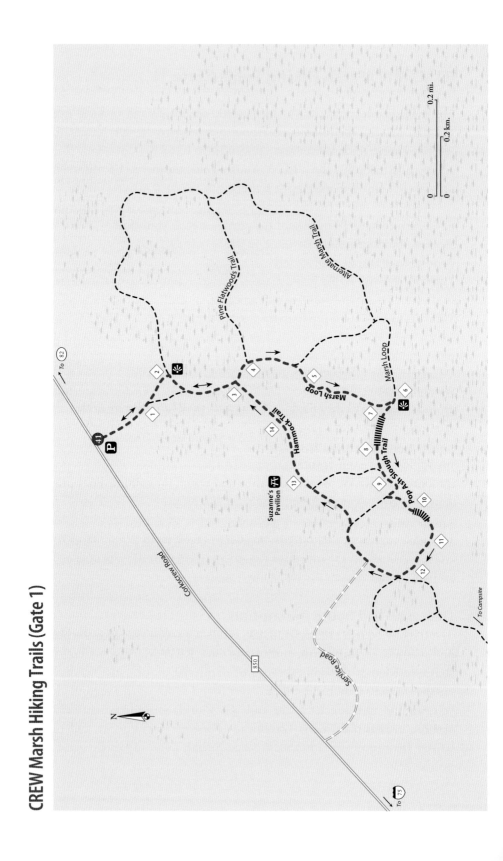

Everglades National Park. Everglades racers and eastern coachwhips are two snakes that can sometimes be seen along the trails. Look also for keeled green snakes, garter snakes, and southern hognose snakes, plus be watchful for venomous eastern diamondback rattlesnakes and cottonmouth moccasins.

Don't be at all surprised to see Florida black bears on or near the trails, especially when saw palmettos (*Serenoa repens*) are fruiting. The fruits of this common palm are among their favorite food items. White-tailed deer, wild turkeys, feral hogs, bobcats, Florida panthers, armadillos, and even coyotes are found at CREW, so take your time and watch for wildlife. For birders there are great opportunities to see such interesting birds as swallow-tailed kites, red-shouldered hawks, bald eagles, and a menagerie of resident and migratory songbirds. Consider yourself lucky if you happen to visit CREW when the pine lily (*Lilium catesbaei*) is in flower because the brilliant orange flowers are real showstoppers.

Zebra swallowtail butterflies are on the southern edge of their range at the CREW Marsh in southwestern Florida.

There is an elevated observation deck near the intersection of the Pop Ash Slough Trail and the Marsh Loop that not only provides a stunning view of a 5,000-acre saw-grass marsh, it offers a grand view of some awesome sunsets. Bring a bottle of wine and chill out for a spell, but you must be back within 1 hour past sunset. Part of the Pop Ash Slough Trail has a short elevated boardwalk, and there is also a large picnic pavilion with tables at the intersection of the Hammock Trail and Pop Ash Slough Trail.

42 Cypress Dome Hiking and Biking Trails (Gate 5)

The entrance to the Cypress Dome Hiking and Biking Trails is located along Corkscrew Road (CR 850), 3.4 miles southwest of the CREW Marsh Trails, and is marked with signage. There is a parking area with a pedestrian gate and kiosk at the northeast corner of the fence.

Trailhead GPS coordinates: N26 27' 22.99" / W81 33' 45.77"

Type of trail: Hiking or biking; geocaching

Type of adventure: Hike or bike on color-coded loop trails through pine flatwoods, freshwater marsh, cypress domes, and mesic oak hammocks.

Total distance: Round-trip from the trailhead—Yellow Loop (short version) 1.0 mile; Yellow Loop (long version) 1.8 miles; Blue Loop (short version) 1.1 miles; Blue Loop (long version) 1.6 miles; White Loop 3.5 miles; Red Loop 2.6 miles

Charts: Free maps at trailheads

Difficulty: Easy to moderate

Time required: Allow for 2 to 3 hours, but take longer if you like.

Special considerations: Mosquitoes and biting flies in summer and fall, but they are usually at tolerable levels. Ticks and chiggers are present in the dry season. Eastern diamondback rattlesnakes reside here so be safe and stay alert.

Scenic value: Excellent. Several loop trails are available that lead through pine flatwoods, cypress domes, and mesic oak hammocks.

Overview and Route Description

The color-coded trail system allows visitors to choose the length of their hikes or biking adventures. If you are hiking, take your time because there will be a lot to see along these trails, especially an array of interesting wildflowers, some of which do not occur elsewhere in the Everglades region.

Cypress Dome (Green Loop Trail): From the parking area enter the gate and keep to the right, following the trail past a cleared area where you can often see wild turkeys and white-tailed deer feeding, especially in the morning. Continue on the trail past the portable toilet, and when you come to the first open, sandy area, look for the pink flowers of the endemic Florida scrub roseling (*Callisia ornata*) and the whitemouth dayflower (*Commelina erecta*) with two prominent blue petals that congeal by midday. Here you also might see flowers of roserush (*Lygodesmia*

Cypress Dome Hiking and Biking Trails (Gate 5)

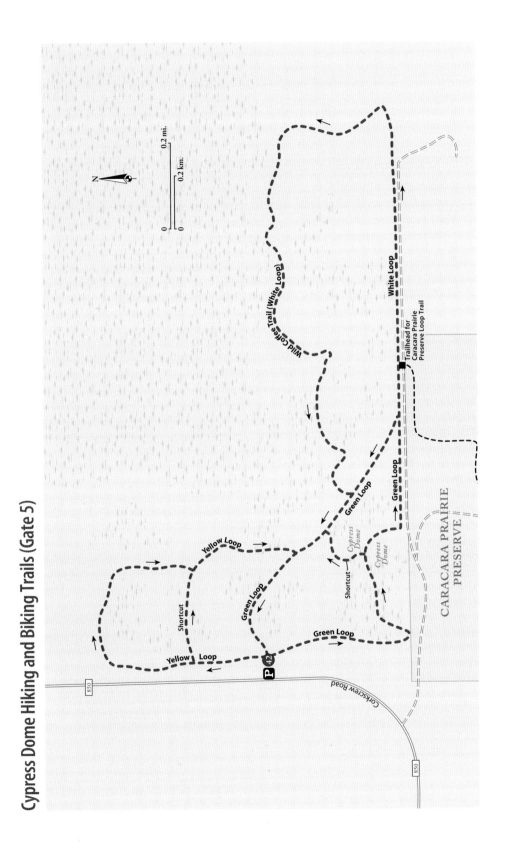

aphylla), which produces rose-lavender flowers on tall, rush-like, wispy stems. When you near the cypress domes, look closely at the ground for the common blue violet (*Viola sororia*), bog white violet (*Viola lanceolata*), savannah false pimpernel (*Lindernia grandiflora*), and Feay's lobelia (*Lobelia feayana*). Rose gentians (*Sabatia*) are also common here.

White Loop Trail: Follow the Green Loop Trail to where it makes a hard northwest turn to the left. Instead of taking this left, continue straight on the White Trail. It will eventually loop back to the Green Trail.

Yellow Loop Trail: From the parking area enter the gate and turn left. This trail leads you north to a bend to the right and eventually bends back south. To return to the trailhead, turn right where the trail intersects with the Green Loop, or you can continue exploring. There is a lot more to see so visit the CREW Marsh in all seasons of the year, and be sure to attend their guided walks, interpretive programs, and special events.

43 Caracara Prairie Preserve Loop Trail

Trailhead GPS coordinates: N26 27' 06.60" / W81 33' 04.23"
Type of trail: Hiking
Type of adventure: Hike on a color-coded loop trail through cattle land, prairies, mesic pine flatwoods, and depression marshes.
Total distance: Roughly 4.5 miles round-trip from the Cypress Dome Trail parking area
Charts: Free maps at the parking lot trailhead kiosk. This trail is designated as the Red Trail.
Difficulty: Easy to moderate
Time required: Allow for 3 hours, but take longer if you like.

The crested caracara favors being around open grasslands like cattle ranches, typically near roadways where they can find road-killed animals to scavenge. They will also attack amphibians, reptiles, small mammals, and other birds.

Caracara Prairie Preserve Loop Trail

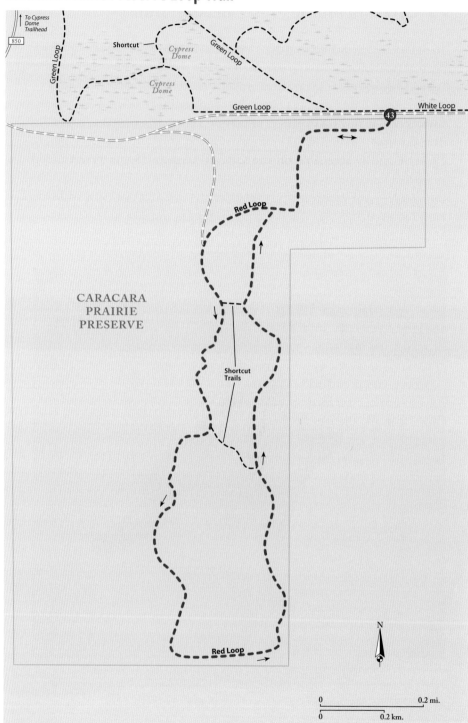

Special considerations: Mosquitoes and biting flies in summer and fall, but they are usually at tolerable levels. Ticks and chiggers in the dry season. Eastern diamondback rattlesnakes are present so be safe and stay alert.
Scenic value: Good to excellent. Portions of the trail traverse cattle grazing land.

Overview and Route Description

This 2.6-mile hiking trail loops through the 368-acre Caracara Prairie Preserve and is accessible off the CREW Cypress Dome White Loop Trail (the trailhead will be on your right about a mile from the parking area; see White Loop Trail directions for the Cypress Dome Hiking and Biking Trails). Because the open prairies in the preserve still serve as open range for grazing cattle, there are occasional kissing gates that act as barricades for cows but not hikers. A kissing gate swings in a U-shaped enclosure and touches (kisses) each of two gateposts, allowing one person at a time to pass through. The main trail is marked with red, but there are two widely separated side trails marked with blue that offer shortcuts to the loop if you have limited time. Along this trail you have a good chance of seeing sandhill cranes and crested caracaras so bring your binoculars. Both birds are listed as threatened species in Florida.

The preserve lies within the US Fish and Wildlife Service Panther Focus Area and serves as critical habitat for the endangered Florida panther. Look for their tracks in open sandy areas, or lucky you if you see the actual owner of the tracks. There can be excellent wildflower areas, especially in the weeks following fire.

44 Bird Rookery Swamp Trail

1295 Shady Hollow Blvd.
Naples, FL 34120

The official opening of the Bird Rookery Swamp Trail by the South Florida Water Management District was in July 2011. It remains practically unknown except for some birding and hiking groups but is definitely a trail you will want to explore, whether hiking or biking.

Trailhead GPS coordinates: N26 18' 41.85" / W81 38' 01.30"

Type of trail: Part crushed shell, part elevated boardwalk, but mostly a sandy or grassy trail

Type of adventure: Hiking or biking; geocaching

Total distance: 12.0-mile loop

Charts: None. This is a well-defined trail so a detailed trail map is not really necessary, but it can be viewed on Google Earth by typing Bird Rookery Swamp in the search window.

Difficulty: Easy to moderate. Sandy areas can make biking a little bit more invigorating than you may have anticipated. Mountain bikes are recommended. The 1,800-foot boardwalk is wheelchair accessible.

Time required: 4 to 6 hours hiking; 2 to 3 hours biking

Special considerations: Mosquitoes and biting flies may be present, especially in summer and fall, but are usually at tolerable levels. Vultures may be attracted to the rubber lining on car doors and windshield wipers so it is suggested to bring a large plastic tarp to cover your vehicle or try hanging plastic shopping bags from the doors and wipers. Some visitors pour hot sauce or powdered cayenne pepper on exposed rubber to deter them. Don't forget to wash it off later.

Scenic value: Excellent

Overview and Route Description

To reach Bird Rookery Swamp, take Immokalee Road (CR 846) either west off SR 29 in Immokalee or east off I-75 (exit 111) in North Naples and continue to Shady Hollow Boulevard (11.4 miles from I-75; 16.5 miles from SR 29). This section of Immokalee Road runs north–south so turn west on Shady Hollow Boulevard and continue 2.4 miles to the parking area marked with signage on your right.

Bird Rookery Swamp Trail

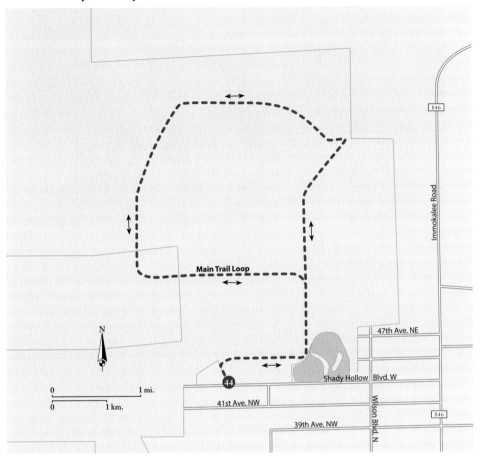

From the trailhead hike or bike 0.25 mile on the crushed-shell road-way to the right turn onto the boardwalk. Continuing straight at this point will lead to a service road that is closed to public access. From the boardwalk continue about a mile to a left turn at the lake. Turn left and hike or bike 0.9 mile north to an angled left turn. Here you can either turn left to loop in a clockwise direction or continue north and loop counterclockwise. If you choose the latter, continue north 1.75 miles to your next left turn and then follow the loop around another 6 miles to the trail intersection, turn right, and continue back to the trailhead. You can, of course, turn around at any point.

Endangered wood storks roost and nest in and around Bird Rookery Swamp. They have better nesting success during years when water levels are low, which concentrates fish in areas where they can catch them easier.

Birding along the Bird Rookery Swamp Trail can be particularly rewarding during spring and fall migration when millions of song-birds make their annual flight to and from their breeding and wintering grounds. Look for a menagerie of warblers, thrushes (including American robins), and vireos along with orioles, tanagers, buntings, and a host of other migrants. Look also for resident birds but most particularly egrets, herons, wood storks, white ibis, and sandhill cranes.

There is a chance you might see some of the other local fauna so keep a watchful eye out for Florida panthers, Florida black bears, bobcats, raccoons, opossums, squirrels, and a variety of amphibians and reptiles. The latter includes venomous cottonmouth moccasins so be sure to admire them from a safe distance. As in any preserve, even venomous snakes are protected. Remember that you are visiting their home so respect their rights as Florida native residents.

Check the CREW Trust website for coordinates of geocaches at Bird Rookery Swamp.

Appendix A: Resources

National Parks and Preserves
nps.gov/parks
All visitor centers are wheelchair accessible.

Useful Websites

FLAUSA.com
This is the State of Florida's official travel-planning website.

myflorida.com
This is the official portal of the State of Florida.

Florida State Parks and Preserves
floridastateparks.org

Miami-Dade County Parks, Recreation, and Open Spaces
miamidade.gov/parks
Department office: (305) 755-7800

Appendix B: Paddling Safety Tips

- Although all canoeists and kayakers are required by state law to carry a whistle onboard, it is advisable to also bring along a flare gun and/or an aerosol air horn in case of emergencies. (These are required if your canoe is motorized, plus you must have the registration numbers and decal properly displayed on the bow of a motorized canoe and have your registration onboard; motorized canoes can be registered at any auto tag agency.) Also consider bringing either a cell phone in a waterproof case or a handheld, waterproof VHF marine radio. Cell phones sometimes work if you are relatively close to either Flamingo or Everglades City, but most will not work in remote areas of the Everglades. The 24-hour dispatch phone number for Everglades National Park is (305) 242-7740. If it is a nonemergency and you have a VHF marine radio, you can try to contact patrolling park rangers or fishermen with VHF marine radios onboard their vessels. Use Channel 16. Satellite phones are another option.

- Emergency situations: If you are in a life-threatening situation or have a medical emergency, send a maritime distress and safety call to facilitate search and rescue. Many marine radios are equipped with a distress key that, when pressed, automatically sends a distress signal along with the latitude and longitude of the vessel. Handheld radios usually need to be connected to a GPS (Global Positioning System) unit in order to send latitude and longitude positions. When the distress signal is activated, the radio will "shadow watch" for a transmission between Channel 16 and Channel 70 until an acknowledgment signal is received. If no acknowledgment is received, the distress call is repeated every few seconds. When a distress acknowledgment is received, a distress alarm sounds and Channel 16 is automatically selected so you can give specific details of your situation to your contact. The signal range may vary, but under normal conditions the range should be approximately 20 nautical miles. Always remain with your vessel near a navigational marker or campsite and try to hail another boater. A red flag or three blasts on an air horn or whistle are international distress signals.

- If you have a handheld GPS, bring it along. Some GPS units have map capabilities that augment the information already on base maps. Regional maps can be downloaded into the GPS unit from computer software (CD-ROM), or some units may even allow the use of computerized map cards (there is one available for the Everglades). With these maps you can view existing waypoints, routes, or tracks on the graphic map, or create new waypoints or routes. There are both water-based (blue water) and land-based (topography) charts available. If you want to be safe and secure in remote wilderness areas, especially if you like to explore areas off marked trails, a map GPS unit is a very worthwhile expense.
- Consider buying a small weather radio so you can keep informed of local weather forecasts. Some are even programmed to sound an alarm if inclement weather is approaching. Lightning kills more people in Florida than in any other state; always seek shelter if you are caught in a lightning storm.
- Bring a dependable waterproof flashlight, regardless of whether or not you plan on paddling after dark. Experienced canoeists and kayakers always expect the unexpected, so if you should unexpectedly find yourself out after dark, you will be thankful you have a light.
- Always bring an extra paddle and strap it to one of the thwarts so it will remain with the canoe in case you capsize. Also, always keep a small anchor with at least 20 feet of rope tied to either the bow or stern. Keep the rope loose so that if you capsize in a strong tidal flow, the anchor will automatically descend and keep your canoe from drifting away faster than you can swim. If you are near the mouth of one of the rivers and the tide is going out, your canoe could end up taking a solo journey into the Gulf of Mexico. To watch your canoe get farther and farther away on its way into the Gulf can be a bit disheartening to say the least.
- Always wear a PFD (personal flotation device; life jacket), especially if you are solo. (It is required to have onboard a US Coast Guard–approved PFD.) If conventional PFDs are too hot or cumbersome, consider purchasing an inflatable life vest like sailors often use. They are very comfortable, and you have the choice of those that you inflate by pulling a cord or types that self-inflate when they are submerged in water. Inflatable PFDs must be worn at all times, but if

you choose not to wear a conventional PFD, it must be accessible to the paddler. Good, conventional PFDs with pockets are convenient because they offer you a place to keep important items on your person, such as your car keys, whistle, pocketknife, nutrition bars, etc.

- Never wear heavy pants (like jeans) or hiking boots when canoeing. If you capsize, you will be weighted down, and drowning might become a very real possibility.

- If you do capsize in a canoe, do not panic (you have a PFD on, right?). Flip your canoe back upright and climb back in. You can paddle a canoe even if it's full of water, so paddle toward shore or shallow water as best you can. Once you are in a safe situation, bail out the water and then go recover any gear that may have drifted away.

- Tie your important gear to the canoe thwarts or consider using a mesh cargo net made of bungee cord that is specifically designed to protect your gear from being lost if you capsize. The mesh net attaches to the thwarts and gunwales with plastic hooks and typically covers about 6 feet of gear in a canoe.

- When camping on chickees (elevated wood docks with a roof) that are near the Gulf of Mexico, be sure to secure your canoe with enough rope to allow your canoe to float up and down with the tide (learn the bowline knot). Tides that occur on or near the new moon or full moon (spring tides) will have higher highs and lower lows than tides that occur around the quarter-moon phases (neap tides). There is about a 4- to 6-foot height difference between tides at chickees located near river mouths that flow into the Gulf of Mexico. Experience has taught me to bring along a pair of small blocks-and-tackle. Tie one to the overhead beam on each side of the chickee, loop a rope through them to the bow and stern of the canoe, remove any heavy gear from the canoe, then simply pull the canoe up until it is suspended safely above the high-tide line. Also, always pull your canoe completely out of the water above the high-tide line when at land-based campsites, especially on beaches where tidal flow can be strong.

- Because full-moon and new-moon tides are higher and lower than average levels, this translates to much stronger tidal flows in between highs and lows, which can make paddling against them difficult, if not impossible. If tides are too strong, simply wait until they subside.

- If you are paddling in a following tide (flowing the same direction you are traveling) and you are in a river near the Gulf of Mexico where tides can be very strong, be sure to stay out in the open water and not near tree-lined shores. If your canoe hits a low-lying branch with a strong following tide, it can turn your canoe sideways and cause you to instantly capsize.

EPIRBS and Other Electronic Devices

If you watched the movie *The Perfect Storm*, you saw fishing boats in the North Atlantic sinking in heavy, storm-swept seas, but before abandoning ship an EPIRB was activated, either automatically or manually. EPIRB is an acronym for Electronic Position Indicating Radio Beacon and I always carry a small handheld EPIRB with me, especially on long-distance, solo paddling trips in the Everglades backcountry. Registering your EPIRB is free at beaconregistration .noaa.gov. Batteries are designed to last five years and there's a test button to ensure it's working. If you are in grave or imminent danger, you simply press the emergency button on the device and it begins sending a signal via satellite to the US Coast Guard along with your GPS coordinates every 5 minutes for up to 48 hours. Help (in theory) is on the way.

Another electronic gadget that I always have with me is a SPOT unit. Once you purchase the device, you simply go to the SPOT website and sign up for whichever services you want. Annual fees vary depending on the services you select. The neat thing about this device is you can set up trips with e-mail addresses of friends and family whom you want to receive a preselected message, such as "I'm safe and am having a great time." When you press the OK button, it not only sends that message to everyone on your e-mail list but also includes a link to a map with an arrow pointing to the location where you were when you sent the message. Now your friends and loved ones know your location and that you are safe and sound.

(continued on next page)

The SPOT unit also has an emergency button that works the same way an EPIRB does except it sends an emergency notification to a Rescue Coordination Center. If you activate it in Everglades National Park, for instance, the Rescue Coordination Center will report your situation to the Everglades National Park 24-hour dispatcher, who will then send rescuers to your location. Like an EPIRB, the SPOT unit will transmit your GPS coordinates and a Web link to view your location using Google Maps. Yet another feature is a tracking button that allows family and friends to follow your progress online in near real-time and saves waypoints so you can review your trip later.

There is another device called SPOT Connect that interfaces with your cell phone to send custom e-mail and text messages via satellite to your contacts. If you encounter problems, you can send a custom SOS message describing your situation, with your GPS position included. You can also post custom messages on Twitter or Facebook. This unit requires you to carry a solar panel to keep your phone charged. The solar panel I use charges during the day-time and then at night you simply plug in your electronics that need charging. It can charge a completely dead cell phone as fast as a home wall charger.

In short, it's nice to have some sort of high-tech connection with the outside world when you are far out of cell phone range. If you think any of these gadgets are too expensive, consider the four football players who capsized their boat 70 miles out in the Gulf of Mexico in 2009. Drowning from hypothermia killed three of them. Pressing a button on an EPIRB would most likely have saved their lives.

Appendix C: Paddling Comfort Tips

- One of the best items you can bring along with you when canoeing and camping in the Everglades backcountry is a lightweight folding chair. On solo trips I prefer to place a low, aluminum-frame beach chair over the bench seat. This lets me paddle while sitting in a chair with a backrest, and it also gives me a chair to sit in at campsites, which is a definite plus! Consider attaching fishing-rod holders to the chair frame by using zip ties to secure them firmly. This allows you to troll for fish while paddling between campsites and also offers a convenient place to keep your fishing rods when they're not in use. When trolling use a floating lure with a lip (MirrOlure, Rapala, Yo-Zuri) that causes it to dive underwater with a swimming motion while you're paddling, but then floats to the surface when you stop. Just remember to reel it in when you enter winding creeks so the hooks won't get snagged when rounding bends, and watch for low branches if a rod is in the holder.
- Keep all of your clothes, sleeping bag, blankets, etc., in dry bags. These are available in a variety of sizes from sporting-goods outlets.
- A stakeout pole is convenient to have aboard a canoe or kayak. They work especially well for keeping your craft in place without having to throw out an anchor. Simply shove it into the bottom and tie a rope to it. There are stakeout poles made specifically for canoes and kayaks—look for them on the Internet. Pole lengths of 5 to 8 feet should be sufficient.
- Do not just pack a bunch of food. Plan day-to-day meals (with enough for one or two extra days just in case) and pack them accordingly. Avoid canned and bottled goods as much as possible so as not to generate too much trash. There are no trash receptacles at any of the Everglades National Park backcountry campsites so you are required to bring everything out with you. The best food items to bring are fresh fruits and vegetables that do not require refrigeration. Consider white potatoes, sweet potatoes, corn on the cob still in the husk, asparagus, squash, beets, citrus, and anything else that meets your fancy. Remove everything from the grocery-store packaging, wash it, dry it, and repack everything in large, sealable plastic bags that can be stored in a dry box. With

fresh produce you are lightening your load with each meal and not generating trash in the process. Nuts, dried fruits, cereal, and nutrition bars are great for snacks. Use apple juice instead of milk for your morning cereal because it doesn't require refrigeration, or use powdered milk. Nondairy, vanilla-flavored oat milk is superb and does not require refrigeration.

• Bring plastic gallon jugs of water—at least one gallon per day per person (more for summer paddlers). Once your canoe is packed, simply toss the gallon jugs around wherever they will fit, but secure as many as possible to the thwarts in case you capsize. Gallon jugs are much more convenient than any other size, and you can squash them after they're empty so they don't take up too much room. If you encounter a powerboater who is willing to share extra water, take one of your compressed empty jugs and blow it back open with your mouth, then fill it with water while thanking him or her dearly.

• If you are a coffee drinker, buy a stainless-steel coffee press. These are great for camping because you simply put the coffee grounds in the press, pour in boiling water, and when it's been in the press 4 minutes, push the filter plunger down to separate the water from the grounds. Voilà! Fresh-brewed coffee with no muss or fuss.

• Because many of the backcountry campsites are elevated wood chickees, you will need to bring a cook stove fueled by propane or alcohol.

• Quick-drying clothes are a good choice for canoeing in southern Florida, both in summer and winter. My favorite canoeing pants are lightweight cotton pajama bottoms. They dry quickly, slip on and off with ease, keep the sun off your legs, and are inexpensive. They won't weigh you down if you capsize, either. Quick-drying polyester pants and shorts (or polyester pants with zippered legs that can be removed to create shorts) are excellent too. Extra-large, baggy white cotton shirts are also a plus, along with a wide-brimmed hat and sunscreen.

Appendix D: Canoe and Kayak Rentals and Shuttle Services

The following privately owned companies offer various services that relate to exploring the Everglades region (listed alphabetically):

Everglades Hostel and Tours
20 SW Second Ave.
Florida City, FL 33034
(305) 248-1122
evergladeshostel.com
Inexpensive, no-frills lodging, guided Everglades tours, canoe and kayak rentals, shuttle services.

Everglades National Park Boat Tours (Flamingo)
1 Flamingo Lodge
Highway 9336
Homestead, FL 33034
(239) 695-3101 or (239) 695-4901
evergladesnationalparkboattoursflamingo.com
Marina store, canoe and kayak rentals, fishing-skiff rentals, houseboat rentals, public boat tours, shuttle services for rental canoes and kayaks to trailheads (no passengers).

Everglades National Park Boat Tours (Gulf Coast)
815 Oyster Bar Ln.
Everglades City, FL 34139
(239) 695-2591
evergladesnationalparkboattoursgulfcoast.com
Canoe and kayak rentals, fishing-skiff rentals, shuttle service for canoes and kayaks (no passengers).

Florida Bay Outfitters
Located at Mile Marker 104 on Key Largo
(305) 451-3018
kayakfloridakeys.com
Canoe and kayak rentals.

Garl's Coastal Kayaking
19200 SW 344th St.
Homestead, FL 33034
(305) 393-3223
garlscoastalkayaking.com

Canoe and kayak rentals, guided canoe and kayak trips in Everglades National Park and the Florida Keys, guided overnight trips available. Locations at Robert Is Here fruit stand in Homestead and on Key Largo.

The Ivey House & Everglades Adventures
107 Camellia St.
Everglades City, FL 34139
(239) 695-3299
iveyhouse.com or evergladesadventures.com

Bed-and-breakfast lodging, canoe and kayak rentals, guided paddling trips, shuttle services to/from Turner River, Halfway Creek, or back from Flamingo.

Miller's World (Glades Haven Marina)
801 South Copeland Ave.
Everglades City, FL 33149
(239) 695-2628 or (239) 695-2091
theevergladesflorida.com

Kayak rentals, fishing-skiff rentals, bicycle rentals, guided kayak tours, fishing guide services, shuttle service (including transportation back from Flamingo if prearranged), cabin accommodations, restaurant.

Outdoor Resorts
100 Smallwood Dr.
Chokoloskee, FL 34138
(239) 695-2881
outdoorresortsofchokoloskee.com

Lodging, canoe and kayak rentals, fishing-skiff rentals, shuttle service back from Flamingo (passengers and gear).

Appendix E: Paddler's Checklist

The following list of gear is offered to ensure that you haven't forgotten any important items.

General
- [ ] US Coast Guard–approved life vest required
- [ ] Whistle (required in canoes and kayaks; keep it on a lanyard around your neck or in a pocket on your life vest if it has one)
- [ ] Paddle (plus one spare paddle)
- [ ] Small anchor (with at least 20 feet of line)
- [ ] Small bucket for bailing (large sponges are excellent too)
- [ ] Bow and stern lines (at least 20 feet each)
- [ ] Waterproof duffel bags and dry boxes for clothing and sleeping bags
- [ ] Flares
- [ ] High-intensity distress light capable of flashing 50–70 times per minute (required by US Coast Guard for nighttime traveling on the water)
- [ ] Orange distress flag (the official distress flag is 3' x 3' and colored orange with a solid black square above a solid black circle)
- [ ] EPIRB or SPOT unit (optional, but a good idea)
- [ ] VHF radio to contact other boaters, listen to the NOAA weather reports, or hail the Coast Guard to report an emergency or nonemergency (Channel 16)
- [ ] Aerosol air horn (three blasts is the international distress signal)
- [ ] Small fire extinguisher (for motorized canoes with gas engines)
- [ ] Flashlight with spare batteries (alert boaters of your position if you are paddling after dark)
- [ ] Two small blocks-and-tackle (optional, but an easy way to hoist your canoe out of the water at chickees instead of worrying about tides all night)
- [ ] Bungee cords to secure gear
- [ ] Waterproof tarp to cover the canoe (keeps gear and the canoe dry in case of rain, even while paddling)

Navigation

- ☐ Nautical charts (Use MapTech Waterproof Chart 28 [Flamingo to Everglades City] or buy NOAA charts, cut them into sections, and then have the sections laminated. Mark them so you will know which side connects to the next, and use a grease pencil to mark your route. These sections are much easier to handle while paddling than an entire chart.)
- ☐ Compass (keep it on the lanyard with your whistle)
- ☐ Tide chart
- ☐ Binoculars (to look for markers as well as wildlife)
- ☐ Handheld GPS (optional, but a really good idea)

Permits and Regulations

- ☐ Backcountry (wilderness) camping permit
- ☐ Float plan (with emergency contacts)
- ☐ Wilderness regulations
- ☐ Fishing license and regulations
- ☐ Vessel registration (required even for a canoe if powered by an outboard motor)

Shelter

- ☐ Tent with no-see-um netting (tents must be freestanding for chickees)
- ☐ Rain fly for tent
- ☐ Light sleeping bag (clothing bags and life vests make good pillows)
- ☐ Sleeping pad for comfort (some are self-inflating)
- ☐ Tarp with supports for camping on beaches (shade)
- ☐ Waterproof ground tarp (slightly smaller than the bottom of the tent so rain does not collect on it)

Water and Food

- ☐ Water—one gallon per person per day (freshwater is not available in the backcountry); up to two gallons per person per day in summer)
- ☐ Water-purifying tablets (if paddling in freshwater areas)
- ☐ Powdered Gatorade
- ☐ Food—with one or two extra days' supply (fresh fruits and vegetables help cut down on cans and bottles; there are no trash receptacles in the backcountry)

- [ ] Nutrition bars or energy bars
- [ ] Raccoon-proof storage—not Styrofoam—for food and water

Cooking

- [ ] Portable stove or grill (consider propane stoves; there is a single burner available that screws directly onto the propane cylinder, but they are a little tippy without support)
- [ ] Fuel/charcoal (consider self-lighting charcoal for grills to avoid carrying fuel)
- [ ] Waterproof matches or butane lighters
- [ ] Cooking gear and utensils (no disposable plastic)
- [ ] Aluminum foil (wrap a potato in it and toss it in the coals)
- [ ] Paper towels for cleaning and starting fires
- [ ] Biodegradable soap with sponge

Clothing

- [ ] Rain gear (umbrellas also work well as protection against rain and sun and as a downwind sail for canoes and kayaks)
- [ ] Cold- or warm-weather clothes (depending on time of year, of course)
- [ ] Lightweight long-sleeve shirt and pants for sun and bug protection (light cotton pajama bottoms are good, inexpensive paddling pants)
- [ ] Hiking sandals (Teva-style) or elastic water socks
- [ ] Wide-brimmed hat
- [ ] Bathing suit (optional!)

Personal Gear

- [ ] First-aid kit (with sting-relief swabs for bee and wasp stings and pain-relief antibiotic ointment for cuts as well as stab wounds from stingrays or catfish if you are an angler)
- [ ] Knife (holstered fish fillet knives are excellent)
- [ ] Waterproof flashlight with spare bulb and batteries
- [ ] Hatchet or, better yet, a limb saw to cut up dead wood for campfires (on beaches only in Everglades National Park)
- [ ] Wristwatch for calculating tides
- [ ] Sunglasses (polarized with brown lenses are best for the Everglades)
- [ ] Waterproof sunscreen (SPF 30 or higher)

- [ ] Camera and film (disposable waterproof cameras are excellent for prints; if you bring an expensive camera, be sure to pack it in a watertight container)
- [ ] Mask, snorkel, fins, and dive flag (few diving opportunities exist in Everglades National Park due to murky water, but fins may come in handy if you flip your canoe)
- [ ] Insect repellent (20 to 30 percent deet is sufficient)
- [ ] Portable weather radio
- [ ] Handheld VHF marine radio (optional, but a good idea)
- [ ] Cellular phone (some may not work in the Everglades backcountry)
- [ ] Battery-powered light for inside tent (bring a good book)
- [ ] Folding chair (short aluminum-frame beach chairs are excellent)
- [ ] Hammock (optional, but great for relaxing or napping at chickees)
- [ ] Fishing tackle and gear
- [ ] Personal hygiene items
- [ ] Prescription medicine (allergy pills if you need them)
- [ ] Biodegradable toilet tissue
- [ ] Trowel for digging a toilet hole at land-based campsites
- [ ] Trash bags

Before packing, spread all of your gear out on the floor and go over each item. If it's not absolutely necessary, leave it behind. Double-check safety gear and gadgets. Always pack all of your gear in your canoe (or kayak) at home to see how (or even if) everything fits. Keep items together that you may need frequently, and pack them close to your seat for easy access. It always seems like a lot of gear, but do not skimp on safety equipment if you need to downsize. Have fun!

Appendix F: Everglades National Park Campsite Information

Everglades Backcountry and Front-Country Campsites (in alphabetical order)

Campsite Name	Type of Site
Alligator Creek	Ground
Broad River	Ground w/toilet
Camp Lonesome	Ground w/toilet
Canepatch	Ground
Cape Sable	Beach
Clubhouse Beach	Beach
Darwin's Place	Ground w/toilet
East Clubhouse Beach	Beach
Graveyard Creek	Ground w/toilet
Harney River	Chickee w/toilet
Hells Bay	Chickee w/toilet
Highland Beach	Beach
Hog Key	Chickee
Jewel Key	Beach w/toilet
Joe River	Chickee w/toilet
Johnson Key	Chickee w/toilet (Florida Bay)
Lane Bay	Chickee w/toilet
Lard Can	Ground w/toilet
Little Rabbit Key	Ground w/toilet (Florida Bay)
Lopez River	Ground w/toilet
Lostmans Five	Ground w/toilet
Mormon Key	Beach
New Turkey Key	Beach w/toilet
North Nest Key	Ground w/toilet (Florida Bay)
North River	Chickee w/toilet
Oyster Bay	Chickee w/toilet
Pavilion Key	Beach w/toilet
Pearl Bay	Chickee w/toilet
Picnic Key	Beach w/toilet
Plate Creek	Chickee w/toilet

Campsite Name	Type of Site
Rabbit Key	Beach w/toilet
Roberts River	Chickee w/toilet
Rodgers River	Chickee w/toilet
Shark Point	Chickee w/toilet (Florida Bay)
Shark River	Chickee w/toilet
South Joe River	Chickee w/toilet
Sunday Bay	Chickee w/toilet
Sweetwater	Chickee w/toilet
Tiger Key	Beach
Turkey Key	Beach w/toilet
Watson River	Chickee w/toilet
Watson's Place	Ground w/toilet
Willy Willy	Ground w/toilet

Note: Some of the above campsites are not associated with the Wilderness Waterway but are accessible from it.

Appendix G: Conservation Organizations

Audubon of Florida
The state chapter of the National Audubon Society. Joining the National Audubon Society automatically makes you a member of the state chapter and the local chapter of your choosing, plus your membership allows a discounted fee for entry into Corkscrew Swamp Sanctuary in Collier County.

Florida Native Plant Society
Annual conferences are held around the state, with informational programs, native-plant sales, and guided field trips. Local chapters throughout Florida offer informational programs and guided field trips.

Florida Trail Association
Keepers of the Florida National Scenic Trail. Local chapters throughout Florida offer informational programs and group outings for members and nonmembers.

The Nature Conservancy
One of the best environmental watchdog groups that purchases environmentally sensitive lands throughout the country.

North American Butterfly Association
Annual conferences are held around the country. Local chapters throughout Florida offer informational programs, group field trips, and butterfly counts. The Miami Blue Chapter hosts Butterfly Days at Fairchild Tropical Botanic Garden each year, featuring butterfly walks, plant sales, and educational speakers.

Sierra Club
This all-volunteer organization with local chapters throughout Florida holds monthly public meetings to inform people about local environmental issues. Chapters also offer outings that include canoeing, kayaking, biking, hiking, and overnight family campouts.

Tropical Audubon Society

Offers local and out-of-country guided birding trips, native plant sales, special events, annual bird counts, and informational programs. Based at the Doc Thomas House in Miami.

Index

Mosier Hammock Trail, 51
Mrazek Pond, 77
Mud Lake canoe trails, 78

N

Nine Mile Pond, 62
Noble Hammock Canoe Trail, 65

O

Oasis Visitor Center, 133, 136
off-road vehicles, 137, 162, 185
Old Ingraham Trail, 40

P

Pa-Hay-Okee, 56
Paurotis Pond, 61
Pine Glades Lake, 50
Pineland Trail, 54
poison ivy, 3
poisonwood, 3

R

Research Road—Hole-in-the-
    Donut, 43
Roberts Lake Trail, 155
Rowdy Bend Trail, 81
Royal Palm Hammock, 32

S

safety, 15, 25, 26, 31, 34, 114, 137,
    147, 162, 180

salt marshes, 88, 90
Shark River Slough, 8, 56
Shark Valley Trail, 115
Snake Bight Trail, 74
snakes, venomous, 4, 6, 24, 46,
    90, 115, 137, 142, 152, 155,
    163, 172, 174, 197, 199, 200,
    205, 208

T

Tamiami Trail Scenic Drive, 139
Tamiami Trail Triathlon, 119
Trail Finder, 16
tram rides, 112, 114, 171, 172. *See
    also driving.*
Turner River Canoe Trail, 164
Turner River Road Scenic
    Drive, 158

W

W. J. Janes Memorial Scenic
    Drive, 172
Walking, 13, 16, 34, 37, 54, 56, 58,
    71, 83, 85, 115, 169, 191. *See
    also hiking.*
West Lake to Alligator Creek
    Paddling Trail, 71

About the Author

Roger L. Hammer is a native Floridian from Cocoa Beach who has explored the Everglades region extensively for more than thirty years. He is a professional naturalist, retired from the Miami-Dade Parks, Recreation and Open Spaces Department, and a volunteer instructor at Fairchild Tropical Botanic Garden in Coral Gables, Florida. He received the first Marjory Stoneman Douglas Award presented by the Dade Chapter of the Florida Native Plant Society in 1982 for "outstanding, consistent, and constant service in the areas of education, research, promotion, and preservation of native plants." The Tropical Audubon Society honored him with the prestigious Charles M. Brookfield Medal in 1996 for "outstanding service in the protection of our natural resources." In 2003 he received the Green Palmetto Award in Education from the Florida Native Plant Society. In 2008 he was the keynote speaker at the Nineteenth World Orchid Conference, and in 2013 he was a keynote speaker at the Florida Native Plant Society's annual state conference. In 2012 he received an honorary Doctor of Science degree from Florida International University and a lifetime achievement award from the Florida Native Plant Society, Tropical Audubon Society, and the North American Butterfly Association.

Roger is an avid canoeist, kayak fisherman, wildflower photographer, gardener, and rum connoisseur. He is also the author of *Everglades Wildflowers* (second edition, FalconGuides, 2014), *Florida Keys Wildflowers* (FalconGuides, 2004), and *Florida Icons: 50 Classic Views of the Sunshine State* (Globe Pequot, 2011). He lives in Homestead, Florida, with his wife, Michelle.

For more information on Roger, visit rogerlhammer.com.

Great egrets strut their breeding plumage in late winter and spring in preparation for the upcoming nesting season. They are among the most common egrets in the Everglades.